W9-BOO-739

We've Come This Far by Faith:
Dr. Pone's Ten Keys to Success

Testimonials

The book serves as an example, not only of personal triumph of a person who just happens to have been born with a disability, it more importantly shows the determination and dedication to pursue his lifelong dream when others, outside of Darrell's family and circle of friends/supporters, were in doubt. Any person who has ever been doubted or had to overcome significant obstacles can benefit from the message. It's a story that any person who has beat the odds can relate to.

Keith Little, MPA
Executive Director,
Queens Children's Psychiatric Center

Wow! What an inspirational story. But, it didn't feel like I was reading a story. It felt more like a conversation with a close personal friend. Darrell thanks for sharing.

Parents MUST share this book with their children. Instead of preaching to kids that they can do anything, here's a real life example how a family's love and faith in God defied all the possibilities. For those who think they've been dealt a raw deal or there's no hope, you NEED to read this book. Afterward you'll feel that there's no end to what you can accomplish. Love and faith have no limits. This story reminds you of just that.

Natalie Hendricks Nichelson
Amazon.com reviewer

Dr. Pone's writing really touched me. His words were so honest. I could feel his pain with all the awkward moments he described while telling his story. I could relate both from a child's point of view and also as a parent. How difficult it is to see your child struggling in anything. I have many times discussed with my children how fortunate they are to have been born in this place in this time to this family. They know how easily things come to them and that it's not always that way for others.

I really have great appreciation and admiration for Darrell's mom, Annette. It takes a special woman to teach a child with challenges to be proud and independent. She really did a great job. I am grateful to Dr. Pone for sharing his story in this book. All parents, even those whose children are not disabled, can appreciate, benefit from and enjoy reading this book.

Judy Martinez, R.E.A.D Book Club,
Morristown New Jersey

⭐⭐⭐⭐⭐ **A must read!**

Very inspiring. Not only is this a must read for anyone faced with a physical challenge or raising someone with a physical challenge, it is also a excellent inspirational and motivational book for all. Dr. Pones' book *"We've Come This Far By Faith"* brilliantly deals with the conundrum of nurture vs nature. It also deals with the advantages of looking at a life challenge as a cup half full as opposed to half empty. An equally important point is that this book is an excellent tool to help people understand that a physically challenged person is not a burden to society, but ignorance is.

Because of *"We've Come This Far By Faith"* I now have a much healthier view of those who are physically challenged. I recommend this book to all, especially institutions that are helping to develop life skills for those who are physically challenged. I deem it a must read for all physically challenged youngsters.

Erskine R. Matthews "Seeker"
Amazon.com reviewer

Dr. Pone, I really enjoyed this book. There is a saying that 'you don't find books, books find you'; and indeed, this book found me at the Meharry Medical College reunion this weekend. Thanks also for the 10 keys to success and the following quotes were seemingly written just for me: **invest in the healing process**; **'in any profession, you need mentors'**, and **'patient care and cure go hand in hand'**.

I am encouraged by the title of this book, and also by the summary point, that **'the positive outweighs the negative'** and the recognition that **we are more than flesh** (spiritual beings in physical form, I have heard) 'spirit, mind and body'. As a neurologist, I am always impressed by those who recognize and demonstrate that the mind is separate from the brain. Thanks again graciously for sharing your life through your book.

Dr. Penelope Edwards-Conrad, Neurologist

Dr. Pone's book is a tremendous inspiration! He has achieved so much and has let nothing hold him back from his goals. After having the pleasure of hearing him speak, I was very moved not only by Dr. Pone as a doctor, but also his sense of humor, his warmth and the wonderful human being that he is.

Paula, Member, R.E.A.D. Book Club

Bro. Darrell, after reading your book I thought that this book should be an inspiration to everybody who reads it. Every chapter was thoughtful and tastefully moving with each journey of your life. I sincerely believe *"We've come this far by Faith"*, should be a curriculum in every school as motivation for all students.

After reading your book I am still amazed by the contributions you made to society. Darrell, you touch my soul and heart, my friend, and I knew I was in the presence of a very gifted and anointed child of God.

Deacon Jefferson,
Congregational Church of South Hempstead

"Dr. Darrell Pone's story is as inspirational as they come. To those with disabilities, of any kind and of any age, he is a true role model. To the rest of us, his story should serve as a wake up call to stop making excuses and get started on the job of making the most that you can with your life."

John Hanc, contributing writer
to Newsday and co-author of
"Racing for Recovery: From Addict to Ironman"

Darrell, I finished reading you book today. Man, it is excellent. I am passing it along to a friend. Thank you for the inspirational mention in the book. You deserve high praise for your labor. I have known you since you were a boy and have observed your growth and maturation over the past four decades and I must say, with all due respect, that you deserve ALL the credit. You have dared to, not only, dream the impossible dream but you worked very hard and you achieved it. Stay positive. Keep up the good work.

Bill Hayling, MD Obstetrics and Gynecology
Retired staff physician; Martin Luther King Hospital;
Los Angeles, California

Darrell, your book was so compelling that I read it OUT LOUD to my husband and daughter as we were driving to the Coast last weekend. Congratulations on being the outstanding person that you are! If your book doesn't inspire someone, they must be DEAD!

Pam Fobbs, Attorney
Past President, NMA Auxilairy

Dear Darrell, I received your wonderful book last week. Congratulations to you for all the great work you've done so far, and for all the work you'll surely do in the future. I thank God for people like you!

Deborah Rath
Your Smooth Jazz Station   CD 101.9

Darrell, your book was a help to me as I have a child with a disability. Your insights into what it is like to live with a disability have shown me how to be a better mother to my child. I have learned from you and I have learned from the example set forth by your mother, Annette. I an on call at the hospital tonight (you know what it is like to be on call) and I read your book while waiting in the delivery room, as I read your book, tears welled up in my eyes. We've Come This Far by Faith is a must read for every mother with a child with a disability. Thank You so much.

Monique Jones, M D – Obstetrics and Gynecology
Long Island, New York

I bought your book last Monday at the Metro Black Clergy Meeting and read your very inspirational book in one sitting book.

Reverend Deborah Dee Brayton

Copyright © 2007 by Darrell W. Pone, M.D.

Published by Pone Inspirations
www.poneinspirations.com

All rights reserved. No part of this publication may be reproduced, stored in a retrieval system or transmitted, in any form, or by any means, electronic, mechanical, recorded, photocopied, or otherwise, without the prior permission of the copyright owner, except by a reviewer who may quote brief passages in a review.

ISBN 13: 978-0-9787650-0-2
ISBN 10: 0-9787650-0-1

Printed in the United States of America

KAMARI

We've Come This Far By Faith

10 Keys to Success

Be Blessed

Darrell W. Pone, M.D.

Darrell 11/30/08

with an Introduction by
DAVID N. DINKINS,
106th Mayor of New York City

Table Of Contents

Dedication

This book is dedicated to:

The United Cerebral Palsy of Nassau County, New York

The Meharry Medical College

The National Medical Association

Dr. and Mrs. Jesse Pone, My Parents

Dr. Gloria Nixon Pone, my wife, and
My immediate and extended family

Acknowledgments

I would like to thank the following for making this book a reality: Gloria Nixon-Pone, Jacques L. Sexton, Joe Watkins, Eleanor Hatcher, Johnny Hatcher, Lydia Geary, and Betty Obiajulu. You've given me love, support, and patience during this lengthy but most enjoyable process.

I acknowledge the Workshops In Business Opportunities (WIBO) for lending us the wisdom and knowledge of one of your very best, Mr. Elroye Jones.

Thank you, Rev. Patrick G. Duggan, pastor of the Congregational Church of South Hempstead and solo leader of the song that inspired the title of this book, "We've Come This Far by Faith." Also, I want to thank Mr. Nigal Gretton, professor at St. John's University and master musician of Nassau County, and the many others at the Congregational Church of South Hempstead who have supported me.

I would be remiss if I did not give a special thanks to Mrs. Lar Watkins, president and CEO of Elegant Events by Lar & Associates. I thank you for all of the help that you have given to me by
- Meeting with the publisher;
- Scanning pictures into your computer;
- Making bookmarks and *Ten Keys to Success* inserts;
- Spending countless hours in your office pulling this project together;
- Lending your superb knowledge in the use of computers.

Finally, for your love and dedication to this project, I thank you.

Introduction

David N. Dinkins
106th mayor, city of New York

I often reflect on my early years growing up in a community of families who struggled daily with the poverty of Depression-era America but who were rich in aspiration, determination, and the will to succeed. The Pones and the Dinkinses of Trenton, New Jersey, were two such families, and the author's father—Dr. Jesse Pone—and I were the beneficiaries of our parents' struggles, their aspirations, and their determination to succeed.

Jesse and I were taught the true meaning of success (as Emerson wrote, "to know even one life has breathed easier because you have lived") and, from the beginning of our lives, were charged with the responsibility of caring for others. Together with our life partners, my Joyce and Jesse's Annette, we were fortunate to have overcome some of the obstacles placed in our paths by virtue of our race to enable us to claim some measure of our birthright and to pass that measure on to our children.

David Jr. and Donna have been the source of such pride and joy to Joyce and me over their lifetimes, and I daresay that Annette and Jesse reveled in the accomplishments of their Victor, Cheryl ... and, of course, Darrell. This book, authored by their remarkable son, is far more than a testimonial to the teachings of his parents. It is more, even, than an account of one man's triumph over the adversity of physical challenge. In the pages of this book, Dr. Darrell Pone has given us insights into the daily challenges of a young man growing to maturity in a society intolerant of difference—be it color, culture, or physical condition—and the role of community in helping him to meet the daily challenges with which he has been confronted in his drive to success.

We've Come This Far by Faith is a compelling depiction of largely unspoken interactions within families, among members of a community, and with the larger society. Dr. Pone has chosen to share with his readers the intimate details of the complex mechanisms that have enabled him to do better than cope with physical challenge—to confront it head-on. He has made this choice in hopes of inspiring others to embrace the gifts that can come with "difference" and to encourage us all to overcome our prejudices and ignorance of the struggles and victories of the differently abled.

Dr. Pone's story gives us a deeper appreciation of the obstacles that will continue to lie in the path of even those who, like himself, have been blessed with intelligence, persistence, and the support of families and communities and underscores the rewards of the heightened awareness and discipline required to contend with an imperfect and often inhospitable world.

When I speak with young people, as I do often, I hope to impart lessons I have learned in part from the experiences of Dr. Pone and others similarly challenged. I ask them not to dwell on the circumstances that may have made their progress more difficult than it ought to have been, although there is much to be said about that. Instead, I share with them my confidence that they will succeed at whatever they choose to be and do with their lives, offer them my encouragement to get involved in serving others, and thank them for giving us hope for the future. And that is the essence of the message of this book. We, as individuals and as a people, have come this far by *faith* in ourselves, *hope* for a bright future, and *charity* toward others.

This was the legacy left by my childhood friend to his son Darrell, and I am proud to bear witness to this fine effort to share that legacy with others. In eulogizing Darrell's father upon his passing in 1992, I shared my belief that service to others is the rent we pay for our space on earth and that Dr. Jesse Pone departed us paid in full. I cautioned that we must not let him look down and find any of us in arrears. There is no danger of that with Dr. Darrell Pone. He has more than met the measure, and we thank him for it.

Preface

The title of this book is found in the words of my favorite hymn. The basis for this song is found in 2 Corinthians 5:7, which states, "For we walk by faith and not by sight." My entire life has been a walk of faith. I placed my faith in God and in my confident expectation that, one day, the dreams and hopes that God had placed in my heart would come to pass. The very first time I heard "We've Come This Far by Faith" sung in church, tears rolled down my face. I relate this hymn to my life, the life of my parents, and the struggles of all African Americans.

I was just thirty-five years old when I began jotting down some of the miraculous events of my life. I thought if I put pen to paper and recounted the blessed life of Darrell Wayne Pone, MD, in the form of a brief but informative testimony, others may be helped or even inspired. I had come a long way from a near-death experience at birth to becoming a board-certified, practicing physician. I have learned and am still learning to lean on the Lord. I have come to love the Lord, who hears and answers prayers. From the writings of King David, we read:

> I love the Lord for the Lord heard my voice; the Lord
> heard my cry for mercy. The Lord turned an ear to me; I
> will call on the Lord as long as I live. The cords of death
> entangled me, the anguish of the grave came upon me; I
> was overcome by trouble and sorrow. ...The Lord
> delivered me from death, my eyes from tears, my feet
> from stumbling, that I may walk before the Lord
> in the land of the living.
> — *Psalm 116:1–9 New International Version (NIV)*

In the journey through medical school, and during the almost-impossible process of obtaining Medical Board Certification, I asked God to allow me to do my best on every exam—especially Board exams that were more than a struggle for me. I learned to trust in God's Holy Name. And as the song goes, "He hasn't failed me yet."

This book is a testament to the life that I have lived and the tough times God has brought me through. As the hymn says, "I cannot turn around." There is much work to be done. After I wind down from my medical career, I want to teach the public about health care practices and various illnesses. No, I can't turn around.

"We've Come This Far by Faith" is usually the processional song in many of the Protestant denominations, particularly in the black church experience. It's a hymn that everyone knows by heart. Many Christians, like me, know the importance of the faith that sustains us and compels us to seek a closer relationship with the Lord.

I know that struggle is a condition of life. It is with great effort that I master the daily activities of life. I am challenged when I speak, walk, talk, eat food, blow my nose, brush my teeth, shave my face, button my shirt, or tie my sneakers. And yet my heart weeps for those who struggled for so many years in the South trying to gain economic and social equality. I cry real tears because, as I have often heard, "Injustice anywhere is a threat to justice everywhere."

In gatherings, large and small, we sing the Negro National Anthem, "[1]Lift Every Voice and Sing."[i] However, "We've Come This Far by Faith" is my personal song of praise; it is my own anthem of glory. The words of these covenantal lyrics ring true to me because I have truly come this far by faith, leaning on my Lord.

When I graduated from Meharry Medical College in 1981, my friends said, "Pone, you are an inspiration to all of us." During my participation in and with the National Medical Association, Toastmasters International, the Men's League at Memorial Presbyterian Church, and the Congregational Church of South Hempstead and at public speaking engagements, I am told time and time again that my life story is an inspiration.

---

[1] Negro National Anthem titled "Lift Every Voice and Sing" was coauthored by James Weldon Johnson and James Baldwin

So, I have decided to share with you, the reader, my journey from birth, with cerebral palsy, to becoming a practicing physician. I will share insights into my life, my disability, my mistakes, and the rewards of a twenty-year career as a physician.

It is apparent to me that in these post–Hurricane Katrina days, where we have learned to expect the unexpected threats of life, we must still be able to see each day as the blessing that it is.

This book is written not only for parents of disabled children, for disabled adults, or for physicians who may from time to time work with other physicians who have a disability. It is also written for anyone who struggles daily to live in a society that is not always kind.

Everyone has a story to tell. This is mine.

My Heritage

Blessings come in all forms, and I would like to share God's unmerited favor in my life.

I was born into a family that afforded me the luxury of three sets of grandparents. Both my paternal and maternal grandparents lived well past the time of my birth. Having so many actively involved grandparents gave us three wonderful homes for the entire family—and often children who were friends of the family—to visit during the summer, Thanksgiving, spring break, and general reunions. We may have been the originators of the phrase "no child left behind."

We frequently visited Illinois, where my mother lived as a child with her parents and siblings. I also remember making regular trips to Washington DC in the springtime not just to experience the sights of our nation's capital but also to appreciate the aromatic smells as the city's cherry blossoms performed their perfumed ritual. This was where my mother's second set of parents lived. Our visits became a family custom during my elementary school years, and it is through this routine that I likely developed my keen olfactory sense that to this day brings me joy. We also spent time in Trenton, New Jersey, where my father's parents and his only sister, Eleanor, lived.

As we searched for more of our history, we found a family heirloom and other articles of great importance, which we carried to New Jersey. My wife and I, along with Uncle John, Aunt Eleanor, and my cousins Sheran and Lydia, sat until the wee hours one Friday night, talking and talking some more. We placed our discoveries on the kitchen table in an effort to bring a sense of historical reality to them. Among our treasures was a little ruddy book with worn corners, yellowed pages, and rusty staple tips bearing the title *The Pone Aiding Society*. Inside the book we found a wealth of information—faded yellowish documents, handwritten notes, old pictures of well-dressed people, and recollections that reached far back into the twentieth century to Alexander and J. A. Pone. My cousin Lydia said this document was originally the property of my grandmother Eleanor, who kept the book among her important effects in the corner of her sewing box. When she passed away in 1985, it became the property of my father, Jesse James Pone. It was an emotional time for us all. Together, we laughed and we cried, each feeling the joys and the pains of the others.

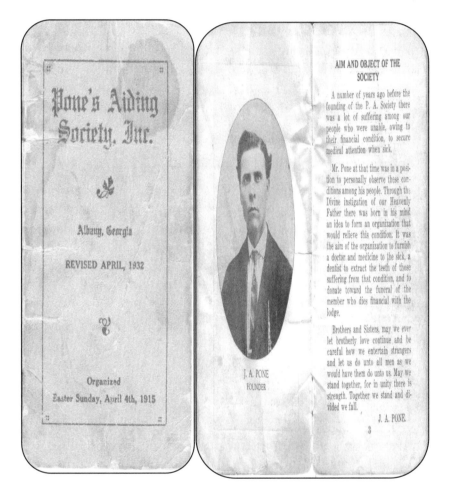

AIM AND OBJECT OF THE SOCIETY

A number of years ago before the founding of the P. A. Society there was a lot of suffering among our people who were unable, owing to their financial condition, to secure medical attention when sick.

Mr. Pone at that time was in a position to personally observe these conditions among his people. Through the Divine instigation of our Heavenly Father there was born in his mind an idea to form an organization that would relieve this condition. It was the aim of the organization to furnish a doctor and medicine to the sick, a dentist to extract the teeth of those suffering from that condition, and to donate toward the funeral of the member who dies financial with the lodge.

Brothers and Sisters, may we ever let brotherly love continue and be careful how we entertain strangers and let us do unto all men as we would have them do unto us. May we stand together, for in unity there is strength. Together we stand and divided we fall.

J. A. PONE.

Yes, I was born into many major blessings on which I had no direct influence but from which I ultimately reaped the benefits.

Below are some of my predecessors upon whose shoulders I am pleased to stand.

Shoulders on which I Stand

Grandmother Thelma Tulane   **Grandfather Victor Tulane**   **Grandmother Martha Ann Weathers**   **Grandfather Reginald Weathers**

Grandmother Eleanor Pone   **Grandfather Jesse Pone**   **Great-Grandfather Alexander Pone**

Dr. Pone's
Ten Keys to Success

My life has taught me many things; however, there are ten keys to my success. I have learned them and used them as life demanded of me. As a result, they have opened so many doors, and by walking through them, with the help of God, I have fulfilled many of my dreams. They have helped me overcome the obstacles life has put in my way. If you learn to use my Ten Keys to Success and apply them daily, they will help you too.

1. Do not let others establish your limitations.
2. Keep fun in your life by relaxing with music, sports, or a hobby.
3. Learn to accept your uniqueness. It is the key to building self-esteem.
4. Persevere through adversity, and complete whatever you start. It will strengthen you.
5. Maintain a healthy positive environment.
6. People are valuable resources. Use them wisely.
7. Develop a plan, or borrow one from a role model. Then set goals and attain them.
8. Learn your craft well, and stand apart from the crowd.
9. Pay attention to your appearance. Many major decisions are based on appearance.
10. Include your Creator in all that you do.

SUCCESS KEY #1

Do Not Let Others Establish Your Limitations.

If my mind can conceive it and my heart can believe it,
I know that I can achieve it.
— Jesse Jackson

Whatever you vividly imagine, ardently desire, and enthusiastically act
upon…must inevitably come to pass!
— Paul J. Meyer, Motivational Speaker

In the Beginning

When I was born, the umbilical cord was wrapped around my neck and deprived my brain of oxygen for several seconds. After a long resuscitation period, the medical staff at my birthplace, Meharry Medical College, did not believe I would live. I was later told they had called the minister to administer last rites. But my mother prayed for me and cut off a piece of my hair to put in the Bible she always kept within arm's reach. Before I knew of faith in God for myself, my mother's faith brought me through an untenable situation.

The cords of death entangled me, the anguish
of the grave came upon me; I was overcome
by trouble and sorrow. The Lord delivered me
from death … [so that] I may walk before the
Lord in the land of the living
— Psalms 116:3 (NIV)

The circumstances of my birth presented a picture of hopelessness. But to a person of faith, like my mother, this situation epitomizes the very essence of *faith*. As the writer of the Book of Hebrews commended the prophets and other ancients, I commend my mother and her foreparents for their faith. This faith is the same faith that I applaud my mother for having and for passing on to me. I have come to know experientially that God hears and answers prayers.

On a recent visit with my Aunt Eleanor, we discussed my birth process. She shared with my wife and me that at the age of six months, my parents returned to Dad's home in Trenton, New Jersey, where my grandmother noticed I was unable to sit upright. Usually babies are able to sit upright much earlier. She was a nurse and realized that something was wrong, and they sent me to the hospital. I was later diagnosed with spastic quadriplegia, a form of cerebral palsy (CP) that affects both hands and both legs. I wept as I listened; yet I am glad I had the opportunity to hear it, because it reinforced how blessed I was and still am today.

In 1955, my family moved to Long Island, close to the United Cerebral Palsy of Nassau Inc. (UCPN), which was located in Roosevelt about twenty minutes from my home. It was there that I received the first pair of braces and physical, occupational, and speech therapy. UCPN is an independent, not-for-profit health agency serving over 1,800 children and adults with cerebral palsy and other disabilities.

Physical therapy involved strengthening and stretching my legs, which in turn helped train me to walk. I remember lying on a huge ball while Mrs. Daily, the physical therapist, rolled it around. Later in medical school, I learned that this exercise was designed to improve my reflexes.

Until I was three, I was carried or rolled around in a stroller. When I started learning how to walk, I wore bilateral, long metal leg braces from my waist to my feet. By the age of four, I was able to walk. As I got stronger, I wore two short leg braces from my knees to my feet. By the age of six, I only had the brace on my left leg from the knee down.

I was given occupational therapy to improve my strength and coordination in both arms and hands. At the center, I also learned how to hammer a nail, use a screwdriver, and develop better speaking skills.

Through the therapy and the loving environment of caring nurses, by the age of five, I was prepared emotionally, equipped physically, and armed with the people skills needed for kindergarten. I continued treatment from early childhood through middle school. Although CP is a debilitating diagnosis, my strain did not prevent me from attending public school. Thank God I was permitted to interact with children my age in school and in other social settings.

At the UCPN Center, I saw children much more severely affected than I. Some were confined to beds, others were confined to wheelchairs, and still others were unable to walk or speak. Many of the children had difficulty holding their saliva and drooled uncontrollably. Some of these children would groan and were unable to make any words. For the first time, I felt stronger than other children. Even though I had difficulty walking, I *could* walk. I never made fun of them, because I knew what it was like to be ridiculed, and ultimately I felt fortunate that I was not like them. Yes, I am blessed to have CP.

Beginning with kindergarten, the Westbury school system arranged for me to be picked up and taken home by a taxi service. The school believed I would fall down getting on and off the school bus and considered this a good solution. When the taxi was late, my mother took me to school. This practice continued until I entered high school, because I was now able to ride the bus.

While I was still in elementary school, Mrs. Rosenthal, my speech therapist, helped me overcome a stuttering problem and also taught me to speak louder. She used a mirror and a tape recorder with me. I was so embarrassed to hear my own voice on the tape recorder. It really hurt my self-esteem. I knew I did not talk right, but now, for the first time, I heard what others heard when I spoke. My voice sounded awful to my ears. This was unbearable to me as a young child. I remember, in particular, I had trouble pronouncing the letter *F*. The speech therapist used the mirror to help me with proper lip and teeth placement. Then she gave me sentences that had several words with the letter *F*. In the 1960s, my therapists were considered experts in teaching children and babies with CP.

In the 1990s, I served five years on UCPN's Board of Directors. Dr. Arthur T. Risbrook also served on the board and is still a good friend. His wife, Mrs. Ida Risbrook, drove me to therapy when I was a child, and now she is an employee at the center.

UCPN
Roosevelt, New York

4th Annual UCPN Honorees
with Robert McGuire,
Executive Director (right)

Darrell as
UCPN Poster
Child, 1959

Honorable Kate Murray,
Darrell, & Gloria

Current UCPN Staff & Clients

My Childhood Years

I was the middle child between my brother, Victor, and younger sister, Cheryl. Victor is two and a half years older, and Cheryl is five years younger. Conversely, Cheryl and I had the classic sibling rivalry for Mom's attention. She was the baby girl, and I was disabled. When I interacted with my little sister, I was still a boy, and Mom taught me that I had to yield to Cheryl. So, we rarely had any physical confrontations.

One of my favorite activities was playing with dolls. They were soft and safe when compared to the bigger, heavier toys and the rough play that is typical of boys. I always chose the larger dolls that didn't require much manual dexterity on my part, so I was never a big fan of Barbie dolls. And for some reason, I didn't like stuffed animals. I didn't share my dolls with anyone, not even girls.

I was always very close to Victor. When we would play, he would make sure he was not too rough with me. In fact, I soon discovered that most children were very cautious not to hurt me. I think they feared the consequences from parents and other adults if they hurt me or if anything were to happen to me.

A stroke of genius that Mom and Dad had was to introduce me to sports. Like most boys in the 1960s, I grew to love baseball. My parents got me involved in Little League in Westbury. This put me with the guys. I had my own uniform, cleats, and a mitt just like the other kids. Of course, I was not nearly as talented as they were, but the important thing was that I was around boys for an extended period of time.

There was practice and games two or three days each week. When I went to bat, the pitchers were instructed to pitch slower. The pitcher on the opposing team did not seem to mind reducing his fastball to a slowball. This might not work in the big leagues, but in Little League it was fun for both teams. As I got older, I realized that the gap between my skills and the other boys' skills was widening, so I was the third base coach and had fun sending the guys around third and in to home plate to score. In high school, I was on the baseball team as a scorekeeper, particularly to keep the pitch count.

By the time I was ten, I began to like football and baseball, and I enjoyed watching wrestling on the television, even though I knew it was phony. Like most kids, Victor played baseball, football, and basketball in elementary school and ran track and played football in high school. To me, basketball was more important than baseball or football, but I found all of them hard to play. I did not have the coordination to even bounce a ball while walking. All I could do was stand in one place and shoot the ball. My physical strength did not allow me to play football or baseball, but I could keep scores, so I did.

We have all heard that men and boys don't cry. Men are supposed to be emotionally detached from their feelings. Normally the covering of the brain, the cerebral cortex, inhibits the brainstem. The brainstem is the center that controls emotion. It also controls the ability to swallow, so that is why I drool and have difficulty swallowing.

In my case, the cerebral cortex is affected by the CP in such a manner that the brainstem is uninhibited and emotions are hard to control. Officially, this is called pseudobulbar palsy, though some doctors refer to it as *emotional incontinence*. With spastic quadriplegia cerebral palsy, I had a problem controlling my emotions, especially laughing and crying. From the time I began to comprehend, I would laugh at any joke, or even if I simply *thought* of anything funny. By the time I was in middle school, I was able to control the laughter. It is no longer a problem.

I was blessed with excellent math and science skills, and from nursery through high school I was given the opportunity to compete with other children. This readied me for college and medical school. The study practices and discipline that I learned early on continue to be very useful.

In middle school, I never scored well on reading comprehension tests. I couldn't read very well either, especially when I read aloud. And I always had trouble retaining what I read. I'm not sure why— perhaps it was due to a weak vocabulary or some other problem. My reading problems haunted me in English and social studies classes, where I performed poorly until high school when I studied American history. Mrs. Silverman was my teacher, and in her class I became an enthusiastic learner.

Because it was too difficult to carry books back and forth, I had two sets of books in elementary school—one for school and one for home. In high school, I could manage with one set. Yet I found school fun. I was on the chess team, kept score for the baseball team, and was on the honor roll. But one semester in high school, I received a D on my report card in gym class.

You may wonder, and so did my parents, how a teacher could give a kid with CP a D in a class that required physical dexterity. Well, one night at a party, my parents and their friends ran into this teacher who had given me that grade, and they really let him have it. The next semester, I got a B. The community really loved my dad, and that made a difference in my treatment at high school. Not only did I have CP, but I was also Dr. Pone's son. I was pampered.

My Early Years

Darrell & Victor

First Birthday

Ms. Doris Webber's fifth-grade class; Darrell (second row)

Kindergarten class Darrell (front row)

My Teenage Years

Middle School

High School Graduation ,1973

Darrell, Dad, Victor

My Father

As I've already mentioned, my dad was a medical doctor in Westbury. Everyone knew Dr. Pone. He was a real celebrity. African Americans had a physician they could look up to and one who made a difference during the civil rights struggle in the 1960s.

My dad was in the delivery room when I was born, and all through my life he continued to be ever present in the events of my life. He was indeed very special to me. I was told he nearly fainted when I had so many medical complications at birth. He was a fourth-year medical student at the time.

When I was brought home from the hospital, he took very good care of me around the clock. He also took care of my brother, Victor, who was two years old at the time. My dad had the vision that I could someday become a medical doctor. How many African American men in the 1960s would have encouraged a disabled child to become a physician? He told me straight up that I would make a good doctor. He knew I had the intellect necessary for a career in medicine, despite my physical ailments.

My father was born in Trenton, New Jersey, in 1925. My father's mother was Eleanor Lee Pone, who was a nurse. Her parents named her Nellie, but she changed her name to Eleanor because she thought it sounded better. Grandmother Eleanor always instilled a sense of pride in Dad and told him he would be a doctor. My father's father, Jesse Pone, was a railroad worker. Dad has one sister, Eleanor, who is still living. Also, my great-grandfather was Alexander Pone, who was a preacher.

After high school, Dad enlisted in the army and also attended Howard University in Washington DC. While attending Howard, Dad met his wife, then Annette Tulane, on the steps of the chemistry building. My father said his heart went flip-flop. He knew she was the one.

From Howard, Dad earned a bachelor of science degree in chemistry. My inherent intelligence and love for chemistry was passed on to me from both sides of my family. My grandfather, the late Victor J. Tulane, was a chemistry professor at Howard University in the 1950s, and my mother earned her master's degree when I was in high school.

After his graduation from Howard, Dad entered Meharry Medical College. During his time there, he was voted class president. He was third in his class in 1955. Dad did his residency at Meadowbrook Hospital, where I also trained. His specialty was internal medicine. In addition to managing, he ran his private practice from the office that was attached to our house. He was also an attending physician at Hempstead General Hospital and a staff physician at the A. Holly Paterson Home for Geriatrics and at Pilgrim State Psychiatric Hospital on Long Island.

My dad was an example of people who go out of their way to help other people. During my entire life, countless people have told me, "If it were not for your father, I would probably not have made it through my illness. Your father brought me through rough times. He was a good doctor." Some of them talked about the good times they had with my father. I sometimes cry when I hear him described with so much respect and affection.

One September afternoon in 1968, we were on our way home from a family vacation at Martha's Vineyard when a voice from the car radio announced that a man was holding a woman and a baby hostage at gunpoint in New Cassel, Westbury. Apparently, the man was threatening to kill himself. When Dad heard the name of the hostage taker, he shouted, "That's Mr. Mitchell, one of my patients." He never drove so fast in his life. Remember, there were no cell phones in 1968.

When he finally reached Long Island, Dad drove directly to his patient's home. He was indeed holding two people hostage. Assuring the police that the hostage-taker was one of his patients, he asked if he could speak with him. The police agreed to allow Dad a few minutes. It was a tense moment. No one knew what would result, but Dad was cool.

Mitchell knew and respected my dad. In a few minutes, Dad was able to do what the police had not been able to do during hours of negotiations. He talked the hostage-taker into giving up the gun. The woman and the baby were safe, and Mitchell was driven to police headquarters. The incident made national news, and Dad received an award for outstanding police assistance.

My dad was an easygoing but firm parent. He never let me use my CP as a crutch. He did not spank me hard, but he knew he could hit me on the buttocks without any physical damage.

I remember one time in particular when Dad definitely didn't spare the rod. He'd left me in the car alone, and I'd climbed into the front seat and put the car in reverse. It had rolled backward down a hill into traffic. Perhaps he was irritated with me or upset with himself for leaving me in the car alone, but that day we bonded like never before. Through my tears, I could see that grown men do cry. For Dad to administer this form of discipline was rare. But he knew that one day I would be the head of a household. He never babied me, and I am better for it.

When I was in high school, Dad kept telling me I would make a good doctor by doing well in math and science and making the honor roll. He knew it would be tough, but he also knew that the profession would give me job security. Dad was familiar with the specialty of rehabilitation medicine and knew that it would not require as much physical exertion as some of the other specialties.

He was very supportive of me when I was in medical school. He always emphasized the importance of keeping balance in my life. He always stressed the need for me to take a break and have a social life. When I was having a rough time, he would advise me to take a hard look at myself and think about how much I wanted to be a doctor.

Dad also encouraged me to always look my best and taught me how to select color-coordinated attire. He loved to dress well. On special occasions, we would coordinate our colors to match each other. He was a very stylish man. In 1969, Dad purchased a black and silver Rolls Royce from a patient. He drove it on vacations, to work, around town, and also when he went fishing.

Dad once told me that the key to his success in life was the tremendous self-confidence he had developed over the years. He thought he could accomplish anything if he set his mind to it. He was the complete opposite of what most people expected of African American men. When he and my mother decided to purchase a home in Old Westbury, Long Island, some of his friends tried to discourage him. But it was his dream, and he pursued it. The house sits on 2.5 acres with a swimming pool, a tennis court, and a stable.

Dad enjoyed working with people. He was more than just a doctor to his patients. He was a friend that they could talk to, and they received from him wise counsel that could be counted upon. Beyond his family and close friends, my dad delighted in the connection he had with his patients.

Dad loved to travel and have a good time. He was always the life of the party, and his friends still talk about how they loved to "party with Jesse Pone." He traveled throughout the world, going frequently to Carnival in Trinidad, and gained a deep appreciation for people of color.

One of his favorite fishing companions was his cousin Marge. Marge Simmons and Dad loved each other like sister and brother. She liked to fry chicken, discuss politics, and go fishing. She could go fishing with Dad and the guys, and she could hold her own. It was much like a game, and she was indeed a winner.

Marge is now a retired registered nurse. I still enjoy visiting her and her husband, Earl, during Christmas. Earl is the quiet type, but Marge and I make up for it. Whatever is in the news, we have the answer. The topics range from Bill Clinton and Monica, to why African Americans do not get their pancakes fast enough from Denny's, to Supreme Court Justice Clarence Thomas. Whenever Gloria visits them with me, Marge and I invite her into our conversations.

My father was well known in the African American community and throughout the country. In the sixty-seven years that he graced this earth, he was a blessing to many people. He passed away June 25, 1992, from heart disease. I never fully realized how popular he was until his funeral. The church was packed, and people lined the streets for three blocks to pay their final respects. Former New York City mayor David Dinkins, with whom my father was childhood friends, delivered the eulogy. Even now, when I think about my father, the late Jesse James Pone Jr., MD, chills run up and down my spine. My father blessed me tremendously during his lifetime, and his spirit is with me as I live.

A wise son brings joy to his Father.
—*Proverbs 10:1 (NIV)*

My Father

Dad, speaking to media after
hostage situation in 1968

Dad, Mom, and Rolls, 1970

It was through the encouragement of my parents, teachers, and the community that I learned not to let others or my disability establish limitations for me. But if you do not have this support system, know that if I could overcome the challenges presented by just walking and talking, you too can overcome the challenges you may face.

KEY #1: People often look at others and consciously—or even unconsciously—assume their limitations. My disabilities were perceived as my limitations, but they did not stop me from pursuing my dreams. What are your perceived limitations? Whatever they are, they are only perceptions, not realities. You have the power within to make your dreams your realities.

* Always tell others how you want to be treated, and never compromise.
* Clearly define your dreams and goals. Write them down.
* Find someone who believes in you and supports your dreams.
* Do not listen to people who try to tell you that you cannot achieve your goals.

SUCCESS KEY #2

Keep Fun in Your Life by Relaxing with Music, Sports, or a Hobby.

Every now and then go away, have a little relaxation, for
when you come back to your work your judgment will be
surer. Go some distance away because then the work
appears smaller and more of it can be taken in at
a glance and a lack of harmony and proportion
is more readily seen.
— *Leonardo da Vinci (1452–1519), Italian painter,
sculptor, and architect*

Sports & Chess

Growing up in New York in the 1960s, I loved baseball. All spring, summer, and fall I played, talked, and watched baseball. My team was and still is the New York Mets. Sometimes they were terrible, but I did not care. I watched them every night on Channel 9 in New York.

I knew all of the players in the majors. I collected baseball cards and traded them with the guys. The baseball card everyone wanted was the Hank Aaron card. By the time I was eleven, I played baseball with the Hempstead Bank Little League team. I enjoyed practice. I would wear my uniform on game days and feel just like my teammates. I knew I did not have their skill, because I had CP, but still I was a member of the team in uniform.

When I came up to bat, the pitcher would toss the ball slower for me. I either walked or struck out, but I had fun. I even coached third base, which I enjoyed very much. I remember one time when the other team's pitcher caught me daydreaming at third base and picked me off. I learned the importance of paying attention.

By twelve, I began playing football also. At first I was scared of the ball, but later I overcame my fear. I was a big Joe Namath fan, and I tried to throw like him. I really enjoyed playing the defensive end and rushing the quarterback. We would count till three and then rush the passer.

I went to football practice every day in uniform. I was in the huddle when they called the plays and then would leave the field as the team went to the line of scrimmage. I felt so good that I knew football and could talk football with the guys, because this put me on even terms with them and distinguished me from the girls. The girls figured I was pretty tough, because I knew a lot about football as a kid in middle school.

Basketball was tougher. My lack of coordination prevented me from dribbling the ball and walking at the same time, but I could shoot from a stationary position. Dad mounted a basket to the top of the garage so I could practice my shots. The kids never teased me for not having athletic skill, because they figured I could not help it.

In our community, even when I was a child, basketball was popular. I was always a Knicks fan, and Walt "Clyde" Frazier was my favorite player. In the summer of 2002, I had the pleasure of meeting Clyde while on a dinner date with my wife at the South Street Seaport. We shook hands, and he was very cordial.

During the summers, we played kickball every day on Church Street, a quiet street in Westbury. Kickball is a combination of soccer and baseball where one player rolls the ball toward another, who kicks it and then runs the bases. The ball is about the size of a soccer ball. I was able to kick the ball and run the bases. Speed was not an issue, because the bases were not too far apart. I played with Darrell Walker and his sisters, Denise and Diane. Their parents, Gloria and Bobby, were very influential in all of our lives.

I had two cousins, Lydia and Sheran on my father's side, who were very helpful to me throughout my childhood. They lived in New Jersey, and I would see them several times during the year. They both accepted my disability and were more mature than many of the children their age. Lydia was very outgoing and did the most to bring me out of my shell. She helped me to overcome my insecurity about CP. Her friends were also very nice to me. Both she and Sheran would teach me the latest dances. We were children of the Motown era, and they knew the words to all of the songs. My brother, Victor, Sheran, Lydia, and I would spend most of the summer at our grandmother's house in Trenton, New Jersey. They would help me with my exercises at bedtime. They treated me as normal as possible, but they understood my limitations, such as fast walking, running, and participation in some sports events. I would participate in wrestling matches on the large bed in our bedroom. We had fun.

I learned to play chess in the eighth grade. My dad's friend, Mr. Lorenzo Merritt, taught my brother and me, and I quickly became proficient. I competed in the United Chess Federation chess tournaments and won a few games. Interestingly, this competition while I was in middle school was much stronger than when I was in college.

Chess was very good for my schoolwork. I believed that if I was a good chess player, I could certainly excel at school. It especially helped me excel in math and science in high school and college, because the logic is quite similar. I think all children should be taught to play and be encouraged to excel at chess. Quiet as it is kept, it is nevertheless entertaining and fun to play with friends and family.

Winning was great, but chess also helped me build self-confidence and become more secure living with a disability. I did not keep up with it while I was in medical school, but now I play the game at home. In fact, I met my wife and got to know her over a game of chess at the beach.

In high school, I found baseball to be much more difficult. The boys were now much bigger, and their interactions were rough. However, I was still able to remain near the game I loved by keeping score and keeping count of the number of pitches thrown. I was soon named assistant to the manager of our team, the Westbury Dragons. At the annual dinner, I was awarded a wonderful plaque, which read:

DARRELL PONE

In appreciation of
OUTSTANDING PERFORMANCE

AS MANAGER OF
WESTBURY HIGH SCHOOL
BASEBALL TEAM
1971–1973

My First Jobs

After I graduated from high school in June of 1973, there was a three-month break before I started college. Most kids got summer jobs through the Nassau County job creation program. Some worked at the park, while others worked at beaches, stores in the mall, or our concert hall, the Westbury Music Fair.

Jobs usually were reserved for children whose parents did not earn the income of my parents. However, my mom decided I needed a taste of the working world. A counselor at the school got me a job selling Fuller Brushes door-to-door.

So there I was with cerebral palsy and a summer job. The things I most struggled with — walking, talking, and writing — I was required to do. In the heat of the afternoon summer, I walked to neighborhood houses to sell my products. When people opened the door, they saw a black teen boy with a speech problem trying to sell them brushes, mops, and brooms. They had difficulty understanding me when I spoke and usually slammed the door.

Luckily, my route took me to the homes of some of my friends, and their parents would often buy my merchandise. This is how it worked: I showed them my merchandise and then demonstrated it. Then they would look through the brochure and tell me what they wanted.

The next challenge was writing the order on my pad and adding it up. Then I came home, filled out my worksheet, drove to the distributor, and picked up my merchandise. I had obtained my driver's license during my senior year in high school. There were two stipulations to my driving: (1) that I wore glasses and (2) that the car was equipped with power steering. I made the deliveries within a week and, while there, tried to make another sale. If I was successful, I would deliver the new order the following week after I secured it from the wholesaler. I worked just a four-hour day, from 4 to 8 PM when the temperature was not too hot. I was paid on commission (I forget the rate), but it was my party money between high school and college.

My second job came after my sophomore year of college. It was more conventional. I worked for Nassau County in an office building doing light typing and filing. I did not make much money, but it kept me off of the street. I was paid biweekly and had party and gas money. After that, my next job was as a physician.

> Train a child in the way he should go, and
> when he is old he will not turn from it.
> — *Proverbs 22:6 (NIV)*

The Guys

I know a great group of guys. I met them in school and am still in touch with them. One is John Rhodes Jr. I've known JR since grade school. We liked the same girl in the seventh grade, we liked the same music, and we shared an interest in black disc jockeys such as Frankie Crocker, Vaughn Harper, and Ken "Spider" Webb, all of whom were prominent on New York City's WBLS. I was at JR's wedding, and he was at mine. I saw him again while I was writing this book.

Then there are the Little brothers, Keith and Kenny. We grew up together. Their father was a strong and influential African American man in the community. The late Mr. Kenneth Little Sr. was involved with the Drum and Bugle Corps of New Cassel (Westbury) when we were children.

Keith and I loved jazz and would spend endless hours talking about it. When we were young, it was refreshing to have a friend who took such an interest in "straight jazz" like Coltrane and Miles Davis. We both liked the albums *Maiden Voyage* by Herbie Hancock and *Kind of Blue* by Miles Davis. The latter album is considered to be the best jazz of all time. The track "So What" is probably the best piece of music I've ever heard.

Kenny Little Jr. graduated from Westbury High School one year before I did. He was always the designated leader of our group of friends. He was a great organizer and extremely disciplined. When situations seemed out of control, Kenny was the calming influence on us. In other words, whenever there was a question regarding social activities, Ken would be the person to ask.

For instance, when we gave a party, we would ask Ken to figure how many refreshments to purchase and at what price. He would take care of details such as remembering insect repellent at a beach party. Most of the guys just thought about the fun time, but Ken was business-oriented. Today Kenny works in the courthouse in the village of Mineola in Nassau County, New York.

Doug McQuillan (Sammy) lived around the corner from me when we were growing up. Sammy went away to college and then returned to Long Island. He is also a huge jazz fan. *Homecoming* by Dexter Gordon and *The Procrastinator* by Lee Morgan are just two of the great albums he introduced to me. The late Dexter Gordon played the tenor saxophone, and the late Lee Morgan played the trumpet. Doug now announces the news at a radio station in Manhattan.

Weyman Watson (Watts) is another great guy. He loves jazz—straight jazz. Watts, Keith, Sammy, and I would hit the jazz clubs in Greenwich Village and would stay there until their 3 AM closing time.

When it comes to girls, Weyman never needs to go out of his way to attract them. He doesn't have to wear the latest fashions or know the latest dances—the girls just love him. He has a natural attraction. I think he knew from an early age that girls like guys who don't follow the crowd. Weyman attended my birthday party when we were in elementary school, and we were also fraternity brothers at C. W. Post College. We have a long-term jazz-inspired friendship.

John Hanc, known as Hanc, was a great sports fan. Between the years of 1984 and 1987, he would come over to the house whenever the New York Giants were playing. We watched the games in the "football room." We enjoyed quoting football clichés such as "air it out," "establish the run," and "hit somebody." Hanc was the only one of the group whom I could convince to come with me to fashion shows. He never lets me forget how much I liked them. He is now a college professor.

Brumsic Brandon III enjoys fishing and hunting. In high school he once told me that he never tried to be cool around girls. He told them he liked the outdoors. I always respected him for that. The rest of us tried to be cool when rapping to girls. Brumsic now is a grant writer for marine biology classes at the Westbury High School, our alma mater.

The best thing about our friendships is their longevity. We met in grade school, and we have maintained our friendship over the years. After we all went away to college, we returned to Long Island and hung out.

The best part of hanging out was the summer parties in the backyard, where we could swim or play tennis. I love our Old Westbury home. The guys were really proud of me when I passed all of my medical boards. They gave me a pool party at my house in honor of my accomplishment in July 1983, and what a party it was. Keith and Kenny organized the committee to plan the party, and Keith and JR headed the group. They organized the food, drinks, and music. They handled the cleaning of the yard. I gave them a list of people to invite, and of course they added to my original list. People came from as far away as Washington DC, Boston, and Atlanta. I'm sure my parents had something to do with that.

When the guests arrived, I could see the look in their eyes. They were really proud of my accomplishments. At one point during the party, Kenny announced over the microphone the reason for the party and then presented me with a cake that said "Congratulations

Darrell." This meant more to me than the celebration at my graduation from medical school, even though that was a special time, too. The exams were really tough, and passing them meant I would receive my license to practice medicine. Many of my family members were there along with my mentors.

When they see me today, they ask, "Pone, when's the next pool party?" or "Pone, don't you have any more exams to take?" We will never forget that event. For me, it was moving and spiritual. I don't cry at parties, but on this occasion, I couldn't help it when they brought out the cake. I cannot thank the guys enough.

I am really indebted to these guys, who still maintain contact and friendship with me. They gave me encouragement all through my life, especially when I told them I was going to medical school. They were there to celebrate with me when I graduated and again when I passed the boards for certification.

Life has not always been easy, but it has been doable. In both the good times and times of great trouble, I have come to know beyond a shadow of a doubt that I could count on the guys. Without them, could I have made it this far? I do not know; God knows. For me the jazz that we shared was our bridge over troubled waters.

In addition to the guys mentioned above, Gloria's nephews—Jacques Sexton, who is now a New York lawyer; Jelani Watkins, who is a broker for Goldman Sachs in London; Sherman Nixon Jr.; her brother Jerrell Nixon; and Cal Williams—all played important roles is our wedding in 2003.

In the life of Jesus Christ, we find a story of successful male bonding that changed the entire course of mankind's history. My connectedness to the guys mentioned above may not have changed the entire universe, but it did indeed greatly influence my world. I am grateful to God for placing these very helpful and most wonderful men in my life.

Jerrell Nixon, Doug McQuillan, Jelani Watkins, Darrell & Victor Pone,
Jacques Sexton, Keith Little, Cal Williams,
Sherman Nixon Jr., John Hanc

KEY #2: You have probably heard that "all work and no play makes Jack a dull boy." Well, that goes for all of us. It is important that we seek balance between the professional and personal parts of our lives.
*   Play games that will develop you intellectually.
*   Choose a hobby that will allow you to express your God-given talents. You may need to try several before you realize which one you love most.
*   Develop physical strength by regularly participating in athletics or exercise.
*   Create balance between work and play.

<u>SUCCESS KEY #3</u>

Learn to Accept Your Uniqueness. It Is the Key to Building Self-Esteem.

At bottom, every man knows well enough that he is a unique
being, only once on this earth; and by no extraordinary chance
will such a marvelously picturesque piece of diversity in
unity as he is, ever be put together a second time.
— *Friedrich Nietzsche (1844–1900), German-Swiss philosopher and writer*

Think highly of yourself, for the world takes you
at your own estimate.
— *Unknown source*

A person's worth in this world is estimated
according to the value they put on themselves.
— *Jean de la Bruyère (1645–96), French satiric moralist*

My Mother

My mother, Annette Tulane Pone, was the center of my life when
I was young. Mom was born in Joliet, Illinois, and had two sets of
parents. Her biological parents were Victor and Martha Ann
Weathers. When my mother was eighteen, she was adopted by her
mother's sister, Thelma, who was a teacher and an actress. Her
husband, Victor Tulane, was a college professor at Howard University
in Washington DC, where Mom received her BA in home economics.
Howard is also where she met her husband and my dad, Jesse Pone.

Mom had a job as a teacher in nursery school while she was
pregnant with me. When I was born, my parents already had a two-

year-old son, my brother Victor. I was born May 12, 1955, while my dad was a senior in medical school at Meharry Medical College.

After a very difficult delivery, I was separated from Mom. I went to intensive care, and Mom went to her room. The nurse came to Mom's bed to give her the medication necessary to prevent her from lactating. I was told that Mom refused to take the medicine and firmly said to the nurse, "I will breast-feed my baby." Much to her disappointment, she could not breast-feed me, because I was too sick and had to be placed in an incubator.

After I became medically stable, we moved to Long Island, where Dad could begin his residency at Meadowbrook Hospital. It was very difficult caring for me when I was a baby, but my mom became an expert caring for a child with CP. She had trouble feeding me, because I had a reduced gag reflex; it was difficult for me to swallow both liquids and solids, because I would start to drool. Bathing and dressing me was also a challenge, because my arms and legs were very spastic.

I owe much of my success to the UCPN Center. They helped to strengthen my legs and improve my balance and coordination. They also worked for years to fine-tune my motor coordination. I am sure that I would not be able to function in the competitive workplace if it were not for the therapy I received there.

During my years in grade school, my mom arranged to pick me up thirty minutes before the end of the day in order to get me to the center for my appointment. My pediatrician told my mom that I had normal intelligence, but I would require a lot of physical caring. I wore braces on both legs, and Mom would struggle to put them on in the morning and remove them at night. When I was a baby, I had to sleep in them. In addition, before I went to bed, she would stretch my hamstrings because they were tight due to spasticity. When I was five years old, my sister Cheryl was born, leaving my mom with three children to care for.

Mom refused to pamper me—while others would lend assistance when I fell, she would insist that I get up by myself. Although I have a brother and a sister, my mother always took the time to drive me to physical, occupational, and speech therapy three days each week. She also performed the homework exercises with me each night before I went to bed. These exercises blessed me by helping my body to become stronger at a very early age.

Physical support was not the only way my mom assisted me. There is a very special and unique bond between a mother and a child born with a disability. Often there is guilt and a natural overprotection, which inevitably causes the child to cling to the mother.

I used to feel very bad when children would tease me about the way I talked and walked. Sometimes I would hear them say that god-awful word, "retarded," and point in my direction. I would often come home and cry on Mom's lap, and she would comfort me. I knew that both Mom and the center would care for me and protect me, because they understood I couldn't fight back. Even today, there are people who still insult me because I have a disability.

I do not recall ever playing with other children with disabilities, but I would have loved to have played in the first Special Olympics held in Chicago's Soldier Field in 1968. As a child, I would have enjoyed competing in these games, where the playing field is leveled.

Although I looked up to my dad, my mom was more than just a parent. She had a way about her that made life bearable under the most tearful of circumstances. When I was a child, no one ever picked fights with me, but they did make fun of me. I would come home and cry on my mother's lap, and she would comfort me. I felt closer to her than I did to my dad. In my eyes, no one knew or understood more about my CP than my mother. Mom worked with me tirelessly and would do exercises with me at home every night. Day in and day out she pushed me to improve on the person I had been the day before. She has the patience of Job.

Both parents insisted that I do the usual chores that any child would do, such as raking leaves, mowing the lawn, and shoveling snow. However, I preferred helping Mom in the warmth of her kitchen more than working outside of the house with Dad. I could physically master skills inside the house such as washing and drying dishes, vacuuming, and polishing furniture. But, working on the car with Dad required manual strength and dexterity with tools, and I just wasn't very good at it. The solid work ethic I learned back then continues to shape and reshape my life to this day.

When I was in the basement watching and helping Mom with the laundry, she would put on Dad's record albums. There was one in particular that she played over and over—Ahmad Jamal's *But Not for*

Me, recorded live at the Perishing Lounge in Chicago. The track that caught my ear, even in grade school, was "Poinciana." I asked her to play that song over and over again. I must have worn out the grooves. This was the beginning of my love affair with jazz.

When I was in college, I heard on a New York City radio station that the critics considered this to really be a true jazz classic. I could have told them that when I was in grade school. Mom played other jazz albums too, like *Home Cookin'* by Jimmy Smith and *The In Crowd* by Ramsey Lewis.

Both of my parents knew I loved music, so they enrolled me in a class for organ lessons and purchased a Hammond organ for our home. The lessons helped me to develop better manual dexterity, and I definitely enjoyed the sound of the music.

But my childhood wasn't all beautiful music. Indeed, my mom and dad had to discipline me for mischievous behavior like any other child. On the surface, one might think that if you spank or hit a child with any type of disability, he might potentially become even more disabled and the incident could be considered child abuse. Yet my parents believed that if a child were not properly disciplined, he would grow up thinking he could get away with anything.

With a gentle flat hand, my parents spanked me whenever they thought I really deserved it. My dad and mom knew that spanking me on my buttocks would not cause any nerve damage. They would also take away my privileges or send me to my room. None of the Pone children escaped proper discipline when they behaved badly. Since I spent most of my time with Mom, she would typically be the one meting out any punishment.

While I was in high school, my mom furthered her education. She earned her master's degree in guidance and counseling from C. W. Post College on Long Island in 1973—coincidentally the same year I graduated from high school. My mom taught home economics for twenty years in Amityville, Long Island.

We usually celebrated Mother's Day and my May 12th birthday together on the second Sunday in the month of May. My dad and other family members would first give Mother's Day gifts to Mom, and then they would sing "Happy Birthday" to me and give me gifts. My mom and I had a special day of celebration that was just for the two of us. That was so cool.

Mom was a tough lady. It wasn't easy being an African American woman, raising three children, working, and being a doctor's wife. I certainly value my mom. It takes a special woman to raise a child with CP, and even more, it takes a strong, loving, and caring mother. I don't think I would have become a doctor without her love and support. She always told me I was better than the students and the people who constantly teased me. She made me understand that sometimes people's reactions are a result of jealousy. Even when I was ready to give up, she encouraged me to stick with it.

Mom was a devout Christian and always told me to pray and believe in the Lord. When I had problems sleeping while I was at medical school, she would tell me to play soft music and pray. It always worked. She was an extremely active leader and organizer in her church. She started a senior's group called the "55 Plus Club" at Memorial Presbyterian Church in Roosevelt. Pastor Reginald Tuggle was and still is the pastor. While I was a member there, I worked with the Manhood Training Program, which mentors boys ages five to eighteen. Michael Bertty, my fraternity brother, is still a member of this church.

My mother is also a member of The Links, an African American women's organization that does community work, and is a sister in the Alpha Kappa Alpha Sorority.

My mother has been ill for the last several years, and today one of my greatest joys in life is to care for my mother. It is almost as if, without warning, suddenly the parent-child roles were completely reversed. Together, with the help of God and my wife, I give back to her some of the love and care that she has showered me with over the seventy-nine years of her life. My mom has so much love in her heart. Her smile still lights my life. In 1 Corinthians 13:13, the Apostle Paul writes, "Now these three remain: faith, hope, and love, but the greatest of these is love."

I love you, Mom.

A man who has been the indisputable favorite of
his mother keeps for life the feeling of a conqueror.
— *Sigmund Freud*

My Mother

Mom & Darrell
July 1955 (two months old)

Mom (top left) with Links sisters

The Pone Family At Our Wedding

KEY # 3: The Creator made only one you. Therefore, no one else on this earth has your unique gifts, talent, and abilities. Make an objective assessment of your strengths, and ask yourself, "How can I maximize what the Creator has given me?"

* Do not compare yourself to others. There is only one you.
* Make an objective assessment of your strengths and weaknesses.
* Work hard on developing your strengths. Manage or downplay your weaknesses.
* Emphasize the things you are good at. Volunteer for these things whether inside or outside of the home.

<u>SUCCESS KEY #4</u>

Persevere through Adversity and Complete Whatever You Start. It Will Strengthen You.

We also rejoice in our sufferings, because we know that suffering produces perseverance; perseverance, character; and character hope, and hope does not disappoint us.
— *Romans 5:3–4 (NIV)*

Success is to be measured not so much by the position reached in life, as by the obstacles overcome while trying to succeed.
— *Booker T. Washington*

Getting into Medical School

I attended two undergraduate colleges. I spent the 1973–74 school year at Howard University in Washington DC as a zoology major and did well. However, during that year, Howard's medical school showed its ugly side, and they told me in the spring of 1974 not to apply for the next year, because I was disabled.

I applied and was accepted at C. W. Post on Long Island in New York. I attended Post from my sophomore year until graduation. To be accepted into medical school, I had to take the Medical College Admissions Test (MCAT). I was strong in math and science, and I was looking forward to discussing my academic goals with my premedical academic adviser. Most medical colleges have a premed adviser. Their role is to help potential students get into medical school in order to fulfill their dreams of becoming medical doctors. This is what they are paid to do, but unfortunately my adviser was not nearly so helpful.

At Post, my premed adviser discouraged me from applying to medical school. She rationalized that my grades were not good enough and advised me I shouldn't even apply if my grade point average (GPA) was less than 3.6. My GPA was 3.24. I was shocked by my adviser's comments, and my father was outraged because we knew of several other students who were applying to med school with GPAs of less than 3.6. At this point, God gave me his own premed adviser.

I realized the importance of excelling in college to get into medical school. It took a tremendous amount of discipline to study even though there were obvious distractions. I missed many beautiful spring afternoons because I was hard at work in the chemistry labs from 1 PM on.

Luckily, I had talked to many of my dad's friends who were African American physicians. They provided excellent guidance. One of them, Dr. Eugene Thompson, had graduated from Mt. Sinai Medical College. I went to his office and had a long talk with him. He encouraged me to apply to medical school, saying, "If you think you are able to handle the intense workload of medical school, then you should go to medical school and pursue a degree in medicine." His advice was excellent.

Another physician, Dr. Arthur Risbrook, a graduate of Meharry Medical School, had been a friend of the family since I was in grade school. He eventually wrote a letter of recommendation from the Empire State Medical Society. And a very powerful blessing came from a psychiatrist Dad knew. I visited him at his home, and he told me how I could relate to a disabled patient. That advice was gold. I learned of a specialty I'd never previously heard about. It was called *physiatry*.

A physiatrist is a physician who specializes in physical medicine and rehabilitation. I knew right then that I would be a physiatrist. I eventually spent four years in medical school and three years in residency learning how to care for the disabled.

When I was a child, Dad had at least twenty doctor friends who visited our home regularly. At the time, I figured that all African American men were doctors and that when I grew up I too would be a doctor. This negated the bad counsel I'd received from my premed adviser.

I applied to medical school during the fall semester of my junior year of college. My dad advised me to apply to his alma mater, Meharry Medical School. I applied to Downstate in Brooklyn, Stony Brook on Long Island, and Buffalo Medical School. Also, I applied to the University of Medicine and Dentistry of New Jersey.

I remember my interview at the University of Medicine and Dentistry of New Jersey. The doctor had narcolepsy, a condition that causes people to suddenly, involuntarily fall asleep. I was shocked and believed that I'd been a boring interviewee! I felt bad. In any event, I was rejected by that medical school.

Downstate Medical School did not even grant me an interview, even though the dean was a close friend and fellow classmate of my father. Connections meant nothing. I was not granted an interview at Syracuse or Buffalo.

I had better luck with Stony Brook, which is part of the State Universities of New York (SUNY) Schools. It is located about seventy-five miles east of Manhattan. Their medical school was new and small and had a freshman class of about forty students. They had an African American male on the Admissions Committee who worked hard to get me accepted. I greatly appreciated his helping me gain admission. I am sure that my undergraduate achievement of graduating cum laude with a degree in chemistry played a major role in being accepted into Stony Brook.

At the same time, Meharry Medical College had also accepted me, so I was forced to choose between the two. I chose Meharry for several reasons. First, it was an all-black school. Second, most of my friends and possibly a future wife would come from that school. Third, it was near Tennessee State and Fisk University, other historically black colleges. Fisk is known for its beautiful women. It is no secret that parents send their daughters to Fisk to "catch" a Meharry doctor. Fourth, some of the professors and faculty were my father's classmates, and I knew they would look out for me. And, last but not least, Meharry is located in Nashville, Tennessee, and I wanted to experience southern living. When I was at C. W. Post, there were other African American students for me to socialize with, but I knew there would be very few at Stony Brook. For these reasons, I chose

Meharry, and I do not regret the decision. I still see classmates at conferences and reunions.

Howard University was the first medical school to call me in for an interview in the fall of 1976. But I did not hear from them until the spring of 1977 when they told me that since I had already been accepted at Meharry, they could not take me. I was not clear as to whether they would have accepted me if Meharry had not accepted me.

Life is a challenge for all of God's creatures. We must overcome the trials that life presents to us, because in them, we find the pathway to personal growth and development. I would like to take a moment to share with you some things I have had to overcome in my life.

When I was in medical school, I had difficulty writing as fast as my professors lectured because of my CP; my hand would get spastic and soon fatigued. Taping the lectures was not the answer, because I would lose time at home transcribing. Sometimes I would get a copy of a classmate's notes, and of them all, the late Gwen Edwards took the best. She could write faster than most people talk. If I missed anything in the class lecture, I would often borrow Gwen's notes.

The long hours of study at night and the early-morning classes challenged my stamina. There were times in school when I thought about throwing in the towel and giving up on my dream to become a physician. I would call home to my parents at 2 AM, telling them I could not sleep. They gave me several suggestions, which sometimes helped but often did not. I would toss and turn in the bed with anatomy, biochemistry, and microbiology lectures going around in my head.

Medical school was draining physically, mentally, and emotionally. The faster I wrote, the more fatigued I became, which made my spasticity even worse. I did, however, see the light at the end of the tunnel. My friend, Norman Jones—who still calls me "The Brother"—suggested I join a study group. Norm, who hails from Chicago and is now a radiologist in Nashville, and I are still very close.

The study group made studying less burdensome and even fun at times. The rationale was that if I knew as much as my study partners and respected their knowledge, then we all had a good chance of passing exams.

Reading about CP was a very emotional time for me in medical school and during my residency training. It is tough sometimes for medical students to study about diseases they or their loved ones are diagnosed with or have succumbed to. For me, pediatrics was the toughest. In preparation for these examinations, I had to focus and become objective and study hard.

Residency with CP had its own set of problems. In medical school I received immediate and concrete results. Every exam had a numerical score, so I knew if I passed or failed. However, taking care of patients was far more challenging and the results more nebulous. Patients do not always respond to standard medical care. I was not always sure if they got better because of me or because the human body just cured itself by natural healing.

The Practice of Medicine

I graduated from Meharry Medical College in May 1981 and began my residency training in PM&R (Physical Medicine and Rehabilitation) at the Nassau County Medical Center in East Meadow, New York. Frequently, patients would ask if I was a physician. I presumed it was due to my disability. Many patients on Long Island probably had not come in contact with a doctor with a disability.

A typical day began at 7 AM. I made my rounds to my patients and then an hour later presented my findings to my chief resident and later to the attending physician. The attending was the physician with the ultimate legal responsibility for the patients. He or she had completed his or her training and had passed the specialty boards in PM&R.

My role as a resident was to have the latest blood work and any other current lab data before my rounds. Also, I had to have a thorough understanding of each patient's disease from a diagnostic, medical management, and rehabilitative standpoint. For instance, if the patient had suffered a stroke, I had to know *why*. I had to know the CAT scan results, how the patient appeared when he or she was in the emergency room, and all of the patient's other medical problems, such as diabetes or hypertension. I needed to know all of the patient's medications and drug interactions, how the muscles and nerves on the affected side of the body would react to medication and treatment, and the expected rate and completeness of recovery of a stroke patient. Finally, I had to know what type of exercise to prescribe for the patient's stroke, keeping in mind other medical problems and what medications he or she was taking.

Within a few weeks' time and if a brace was required, I had to know the proper one to prescribe. Prescribing a brace is simply stating what the brace should do or not do—what components the brace should have, how high up on the leg it would fit, what joints should be included within the brace (knee, ankle, etc.), when it should be worn, and how it should be properly maintained.

Normally, we would have phlebotomists draw the blood in the morning. Sometimes I had to draw blood, and this is a difficult procedure for people who are not spastic. It was even more difficult for me. Some patients would say, "Doc, I don't have any more blood left for you to draw."

After my rounds, I would get a new admission or go to the clinic, where neck, shoulder, knee, and back pain were treated. Sometimes I would speak with a patient's family to discuss prognosis and discharge plans. Typically, I would go home at 5 PM.

Every week the entire rehabilitation team would engage in a detailed discussion of approximately five patients, reviewing all their needs. There were usually representatives from five or six different disciplines at the team meeting (doctors, nurses, therapists, social workers, etc.). There was a mountain of paperwork. It is easier today with computers, but when I trained, we had to handwrite the history, the results of the physical examination, all of the diagnoses, the proposed treatment plans, the therapy, the medications, and the prognosis.

On top of all that, we would often have to complete patient insurance forms. Nowadays, insurance companies have a clause that states it is perjury for the physicians to knowingly complete the forms incorrectly. For instance, if I deem that a patient cannot walk for more than five minutes and someone finds that patient walking for twenty minutes, I may be guilty of perjury. With so many forms, we don't have a chance to think about how much is riding on each response.

When I worked at Elmhurst Hospital in Queens, New York, the patients were multicultural. Accordingly, I used interpreters for all but my Spanish-speaking patients, with whom I was able to converse. The problem with interpreters is that they aren't always able to translate verbatim what is being said and may not ask the patient precisely the question the doctor has asked. As a result, the patient's response is not accurate. For instance, if I said, "Ask the patient if his *shoulder* hurts," the interpreter might turn to the patient and say, "Does your *arm* hurt?" The patient therefore answers the interpreter's question and not mine. So I must ask my questions repeatedly to make sure the interpreter and I are on the same page.

But stroke patients are not always able to speak and instead must communicate using gestures. Moreover, some have difficulty understanding what is being told to them. Unfortunately, it was hard to determine if the communication problem was due to my speech impairment or the result of their stroke. Their stroke would sometimes leave them quite emotional, and again, I could not discern if this response was due to my cerebral palsy.

At Elmhurst Hospital, I was an assistant attending. As such, one of my responsibilities was to supervise my residents. But I still had my own patients too. I would see one of my patients, then see a patient with the resident, and then see patients in the clinics from 9 AM to 2 PM. And we were often exhausted by the time lunch rolled around. Occasionally there was a late conference, but I would usually leave the hospital by 5 PM. For me, 7 AM to 5 PM was a very long day.

As a physiatrist, I had to relate patients' symptoms to their function. For instance, does shoulder pain get worse when the patient combs his hair or when he puts on a shirt? Does back pain worsen with sitting, standing, walking, or even praying on their knees? This all relates to the cause and treatment of the pain.

Very often a patient's vocation will worsen his or her pain, in which case we did an analysis of potential worksite adjustments. *Ergonomics* is the term we use to describe the adjustment of objects at the workplace to reduce pain. You may have seen mouse pads with an elevation for the wrists to alleviate carpal tunnel syndrome. Other examples of ergonomics include back pillows, footrests, and desk- and seat-height adjustments to help reduce back pain. This is particularly what I enjoy about this specialty—we improve the patients' ability to function.

The biggest problem I encountered was a lack of stamina. Often I was on my feet two hours straight. The faster I worked, the more tired I would become and the slower I would work. It was a vicious circle.

Also, my speech is not very clear, and patients often had difficulty understanding me, especially when I was tired. Often, I would have to repeat what I said to patients, and this would become frustrating.

The attending physicians would drill us about the management of patients and ask questions to test our knowledge of medicine. This is standard practice, and I think it makes residents better physicians. Yet although I was able to draw blood from patients, I was never able to start an intravenous line. Thank goodness we worked as a team.

What about being "on call"? With internal medicine, it was every fourth night. I tried to hang in there initially, but soon the supervising physicians realized this was not in the best interest of the team. They dismissed me at midnight, and I returned to duty at 8 AM. I had three months on this rotation. Luckily, my specialty was rehabilitation medicine and the on call was much lighter.

After residency, the practice of medicine presented its own challenges for me to overcome. On one occasion, I saw a woman in the office who refused to let me examine her after hearing my speech pattern. I told her I was board-certified in the field. I had to overcome her lack of trust in me. During my practice, I had never seen a patient act this way. I was very frustrated and annoyed. Only after her husband comforted and reassured her would she let me examine her.

Once, when I was walking down my own street in Old Westbury, New York, a police officer stopped me and asked me to get into his car. He thought I was drunk, based on the way I was walking. I told him I had CP, and although he did not give me a sobriety test, he made me get into the squad car and refused to let me walk home. I had been living there for over ten years. Not many blacks live in our neighborhood. He may not have believed me.

When some people see me—an African American male with a disability—they find it hard to believe I'm a physician. I've been asked, "Are you a doctor?" Usually the white coat, the name badge, the stethoscope, and the confident manner in which I speak are dead giveaways, but not always.

When there is a question or a concern, I spend the time necessary to address it, no matter how slight it may seem. With authority, I speak directly to the issue in a manner designed to put the patient at ease and be instructive at the same time. Most patients, both male and female, regardless of their different mores, admire my accomplishments as a doctor.

We all know the stigma of doctors' handwriting. We had to write fast in college and medical school. When I started medical school in 1977, there were few laptop computers. There was so much material to write in the lectures that I wrote fast so I would not miss anything and thus avoid failing an exam. In my residency training, I saw many patients and attended more lectures, so I still wrote fast. The faster I wrote, the more illegible my writing became. However, I have always been able to read any physician's handwriting. I mentioned above that I always wrote orders neatly, and some even said my writing was better than that of other doctors.

In my opinion, doctors' handwriting jokes are in bad taste. They can show a lack of compassion and understanding. Being born with CP, I experienced children and teachers who insulted my handwriting. Believe it or not, some health-care professionals still act like children and insult my penmanship. People see that I am disabled. People think I write poorly because I'm a physician. But do they think I talk and walk a certain way because I am a physician? Of course not! They make insensitive jokes about my penmanship and then tell me what an inspiration I am to others. The things about me that inspire them are the same things that cause poor penmanship.

In view of this situation, I have written letters to the editor of the *Journal of the National Medical Association*. I have also given notice to a branch of the federal government about gutless and cowardly remarks that I hear come from the lips of so-called medical professionals. It is hard for me to hold a pen and hard for me to write, and as a result, it is hard for me and others to read my handwriting. I guess life is hard. Sometimes this matter is hard for me to deal with.

It is tough to distinguish children's behavior from the childlike behavior of adults. I have yelled at staff about this issue also. Then they stop. Asking them in a mild manner to cease from penmanship jokes does not stop the jokes, so I have to become more forceful. I pray that people in general will develop more wisdom and insight into dealing with people who are different from themselves. It would be helpful, to me, if people simply ask me why my writing is poor before they make comments.

There are other challenges I face that cause people to make unkind remarks. Buttoning the top button of a dress shirt, for example, is difficult, if not impossible, because my hand coordination simply cannot make the moves necessary to accomplish this routine task. Yet others who know of my affliction have ridiculed me for looking unprofessional when my top button is open. I don't believe being disabled makes one unprofessional. However, to overcome this challenge, I bought a hook in order to button the top of my shirt. Neatness has always been an area of weakness for me.

In other areas, CP has a social effect. I sometimes drool when I speak or chew. The main problem is that when people see me do anything that they think is inappropriate, they think they know whether it is due to my cerebral palsy or not, and they usually do not ask. I realize that talking to me about my disability may be difficult for some people. Fortunately, most patients don't make the silly handwriting jokes, nor do they make fun of shirt buttons that are left unbuttoned. I must continue to pray for those who may enjoy making light of persons who are disabled. In my prayers, I call upon God to show them the error of their ways and to help them to stop the abusive behavior.

I am very often totally bewildered when the same people who consider me an inspiration turn on me with massive criticism. For example, I worked at a New York hospital for a number of years. The staff of medical professionals gave me a large plaque that praised me and cited me as a great source of inspiration. Yet before the week was over, this same group of people was back to their old ways of using subordinating and denigrating language toward me that insulted my penmanship and how I dressed.

For a person with CP, the activities of daily living are most challenging, and yet I endure them and much more. I have suffered much by the actions of others in both their words and their deeds. If I truly am an inspiration to people, then to God be the glory. In its entirety, my life hinges on the unmerited favor of God, from birth until now, both in the good times and in the bad times. It is written that suffering will, in due time, produce character.

Concerning suffering, the Bible says that:

> We rejoice in our sufferings because we know that suffering produces perseverance, perseverance produces character and character produces hope. And hope does not disappoint us because God has poured out His love into our hearts by the Holy Spirit, whom He has given us. — *Romans 5:3–5 (NIV)*

Dreams Do Come True!

Meharry Graduation

Our Wedding Day

About Cerebral Palsy

Cerebral palsy is a nonprogressive motor disorder that occurs in the developing brain. Usually, this disorder is diagnosed by age one. The keyword is *nonprogressive*. CP is clearly not a specific disease, rather a collection of disorders with some common features.

The most common causes for CP include prematurity, ischemia (decreased blood supply to the brain), hyperbilirubinemia (a buildup of a product of red blood cell breakdown), and external and internal trauma. With better care in the neonatal intensive care units for infants with low birth weight, the survival rate has improved, and therefore there has been an increase in the prevalence of CP. It is estimated that between 1960 and 1986, CP increased by approximately 20 percent in the United States. There are several different types of CP that have been well documented along with the type I have:

Spastic Quadriplegia—This is the type I have. It means spasticity of arms and legs, seizures, slurred speech, and usually mental retardation. These patients walk with an assistive device if they have adequate use of their arms.

Spastic Diplegia—This is spasticity in both legs and adequate control of arms; some people have intellectual defects. These patients usually will walk if they are able to sit independently by two years of age.

Spastic Hemiplegia—One leg and one arm are spastic on the same side of the body; these patients usually walk. They can ignore the involved arm and decreased sensation on that side. These children usually become independent in self-care.

Athetosis—This type of CP means slow, wormlike movement of the fingers, toes, and face. Patients with athetosis have problems with chewing and swallowing, drooling, and slurred speech. These children can usually walk.

There are aspects of CP that should be noted. The brain is immature. That is the nature of CP. In the developing fetus, the last system to mature is the central nervous system (the brain and the spinal cord).

If a neurologist were to examine me, he or she would find infantile reflexes. For example, my toes spread when the bottom of my foot is scraped—this is called the "Babinski reflex." When I sit and lift my heel off the ground, my leg will bounce up and down—this is called "clonus."

In the normal adult, these infantile reflexes are inhibited during childhood by an intact cerebral cortex (the brain covering). That is why normal adults do not have the above-mentioned reflexes. CP damaged my cerebral cortex, so these reflexes are not inhibited and are continued from birth. For the same reason, I cannot always stop the urge to cry, because the cerebral cortex cannot inhibit this urge. This is a part of the neurology that doctors learn in medical school.

This immaturity of my brain has several social ramifications. Most of my teen and adult life, I have developed crushes on girls and women. Most teens develop a crush on one of their teachers, but they also have girlfriends in school. I never had a girlfriend until I was in my last year of college. Until I met Gloria, I habitually developed crushes on women and fantasized that they were my girlfriends. I believe this caused a problem for me when I have wanted to develop serious relationships with women. It was difficult for me to work with nurses, female doctors, secretaries, and therapists, because I developed a crush on all of them.

I disguised my feelings with the use of humor, and the objects of my affection merely thought I was a harmless flirt. In one office, there were so many attractive women I overcompensated by not flirting with anyone. They probably thought I was a loner. Now that I am married to Gloria, I don't flirt with or develop crushes on any women.

There are differences between the type of CP I have, which is birth-onset, and that of people who develop disabilities during adulthood. As a doctor, I have treated patients with adult-onset disabilities. For the most part, my patients were physically normal at one time. The therapy is geared toward getting them back as close as possible to pre-injury level. When they interact with the public, they might be aware of the public's attitude toward disabled people from their own experience pre-injury. They once perceived the world as a non-disabled person. I cannot relate to them on that level, as I have always had CP. I have never interacted with the world as a non-disabled person.

I have never treated babies with CP, and I have little training in this area. And there are adults with CP-induced mental retardation whose ailments and impairments I could only partially alleviate. At times, I realize that my own experience may not help me relate fully to my patients, but I have found that I can provide important guidance to them regarding their interaction with the public during their time of disability. They clearly have to be prepared for the prejudices of people who have no experience in dealing with disabled people. Even if I were not a physician, I would learn as much as I could about CP. People should learn all they can about their diagnosis or condition so they can better help others understand their strengths and limitations.

Because I have a unique understanding of patients' disabilities, I can successfully help them to become rehabilitated as much as is physically possible. I am also able to help them handle their emotional response to their disability and the frustrations they feel when they are no longer able to perform physically as they would like. For example, I teach them to be patient with themselves and accept themselves as a person.

When people see me, they probably do not know my diagnosis, nor do they ask. I often wonder why, and out of curiosity, sometimes I will broach the subject. They usually respond by saying that they don't want to hurt my feelings. Once, a child asked me why I walk the way I do, and I told her it was because I have a brain disease.

We want our children to become doctors or lawyers and enter occupations where intelligence is required. Then, we should teach them to seek information by asking questions. If someone asked me, "Dr. Pone, why do you walk like that?" I would have a great deal of respect for that person. Most persons who are disabled want to educate people about their disabilities.

I once went to a sports bar to watch Monday Night Football. I told the doorman of my disability and advised him that I may appear inebriated even when I'm stone-cold sober. I then asked that he not throw me out of the bar in the fourth quarter because he thinks I'm drunk when in fact I'm merely excited. He understood, and that was the end of that.

In keeping with the football theme, a very interesting thing happened to me just prior to a buddy's Super Bowl party in 2000. My friend, who is of European descent, invited me to his home on Long

Island to watch the game. But even though we were pretty good friends, I'd never been to his home before and ended up going to the wrong house. I had brought some beer with me in a beer box so it would be easy for me to carry. When I walked up to the house I believed to be his, a European woman opened the door, saw me with my beer box, and slammed the door in my face. Luckily, I saw some people in the street who directed me to my buddy's home, but I couldn't help but feel for this obviously frightened woman. Imagine: she opens the door to an African American man staggering toward her with a case of beer.

Later that evening, I wrote her a letter explaining that I have CP and was not drunk. When I went back to her home and tried to put the letter in her mailbox, she saw me and opened her door. We talked and parted on good terms. I don't think I ever told her I was a physician.

I remember another incident where I was at a party and speaking with a woman who unfortunately had a rather condescending attitude toward me. It could have been my race, my disability, or both. She told me her occupation and asked me if I had a job. When I told her I was a physician, her face hit the floor. She stumbled for the right words and asked me about my specialty. After that, the remainder of the conversation was unremarkable. Sometimes people are surprised to learn that I am both African American *and* a physician. This works differently for different people.

On Professional Conduct

In the state of New York there is a division of state called the Office of Professional Misconduct (OPMC). Their duty is to discipline any physician who is deemed to be unprofessional. They have a list of charges that they refer to as misconduct. This includes offenses such as assaulting a patient, writing prescriptions for too many narcotics, and fraudulent billing.

Even though I have trouble with penmanship, I made sure I wrote legible orders for nurses and prescriptions for the pharmacy. At no time was a patient's care compromised because of my handwriting. In 1999, when I had my own practice, I purchased a laptop computer through which I could type my notes rather than writing them by hand.

In 2000 I received a phone call in which I was told I was being investigated for professional misconduct because I was "too impaired" to practice medicine. This was despite my have been in practice for more than nineteen years and successfully serving thousands of satisfied patients.

An insurance company investigator had filed this complaint with OPMC. This was the most ridiculous thing I had ever witnessed in my career. I hired an attorney, who wrote a strong letter voicing his displeasure in their accusations. He threatened to contact several civil rights organizations. I did not hear from OPMC again until one year later.

In 2001 they wanted to review six of my charts. I complied by law and sent them copies of my records. I couldn't understand how a state-run organization could accuse a physician of being impaired without ever seeing him in person. Some members of the National Medical Association (NMA) told me that some state medical offices target African American physicians for so-called misconduct. And now it felt as though I was being punished for becoming a doctor with CP.

In October of 2004 I got a phone call at home from a woman who told me she was an OPMC investigator. She scheduled an interview to discuss how I practiced medicine, and we agreed on the time and date. The night before the scheduled meeting, in which I was going to be evaluated in person, she canceled. Remember, it had been four years, and no one had discussed the accusation with me. Now, instead of meeting with me in person, they scheduled a telephone conference meeting for November 4 at 10 AM, which was two weeks later. I was unsure how they would evaluate the complaint of being "too impaired" without seeing me in person, but my attorney nevertheless set a small office aside for the conference call. When we called the investigator, we were astonished to learn that the phone meeting was not on her calendar. By this time, four years had passed, in which time OPMC did not schedule one meeting with me in person. Nor had they sent me written notice.

When we finally did get a chance to speak, the first thing out of the investigator's mouth was, "Your handwriting is terrible. I cannot make it out." To me, she sounded like a child making fun of me in a classroom. My physician had submitted a written report to OPMC, but the woman had no compassion for the fact that I was born with CP. I was shocked, insulted, and taken aback that the Office of *Professional* Misconduct would be so *unprofessional*. Time and time again during the interview, she criticized my handwriting. My attorney tried to calm her by telling her that I now use preprinted forms that allow me to check off boxes rather than write extensive reports.

A more appropriate OPMC statement would have been, "Dr. Pone, we are aware you have cerebral palsy and therefore find it difficult to write legibly." Instead, OPMC insulted me in the presence of my wife. Their conduct was a put-down not only to me but to disabled persons everywhere. To insult a physically disabled person is analogous to using the N-word when talking to African Americans or the B-word when referring to a woman. I feel very strongly about this position.

During the phone conference meeting with OPMC, I was careful to explain every note in each file using the very specific professional language I had been taught in medical school and in the twenty years of medical practice that followed. Questions were fired at me, and without hesitation, I answered each one of them in detail and with clarity in a manner that, I believe, would have pleased my mentors: Dr. Lawrence Friedman, Dr. Herbert Thornhill, and Dr. Jerry Weissman.

For no apparent reason, the OPMC representative asked for a break and did not return to the meeting as she had agreed to do. Later in the day, during a phone call from my attorney to OPMC, the investigator and my lawyer's assistant argued extensively about whether I should make a personal appearance. We will wait and see what our attorney and the head of OPMC can work out. I believe I will not have to lower my self-respect and speak with them again. Their written apology would be acceptable.

My dealings with OPMC remind me of when I failed gym class or when children and adults made fun of me just because they could. However, all such obstacles have only served to make me stronger and stronger.

Everyone should stand for something. I resent anyone insulting me because of my cerebral palsy. It does not matter if it is a patient, a doctor, the New York State Department of Health, or the Office of Professional Misconduct.

A man who does not stand for something will fall for anything.

KEY # 4: Often when we are challenged and things get really tough, we want to give up. However, when we keep our eyes on the prize, on our dreams and goals, we gain strength that we did not know we had and are able to overcome the obstacle and reach our destinations.

* Do not allow mistakes to stop you.
* Learn from your mistakes. It will save you lots of time and effort.
* Realize that it is okay to be disappointed, but you must remain focused on the goal.
* Finish whatever you start. If you quit before you finish, you will never realize your potential.
* Skills that you develop doing something you don't particularly like can be transferred to something you do like.

SUCCESS KEY #5

Maintain a Healthy Positive Environment.

Two names for negative people are:
"toxic people" and "dream crushers."
— *Jim Rohn, International Motivational Speaker*

Martha's Vineyard

Lying just off the coast of Massachusetts, Martha's Vineyard Island (affectionately referred to as "the Vineyard") is a wonderful spot that has traditionally been a vacation area for the middle and upper classes. My parents and their friends have vacationed there for the past forty years or more. Initially, they rented homes for the last two or three weeks of August though the Labor Day weekend, but now many of them own homes there.

My family first went to the Vineyard in 1964 when I was in elementary school. I didn't realize at the time that it would ultimately be an important reason why I am a physician today. There were many other children my age vacationing on the Vineyard. We often played with them on the beach. One girl in particular, Deidre, also known as Dee Dee, was my close friend. Her dad, Mr. Hilton, was an attorney in New Jersey. Dee Dee was a very good student and extremely bright. She was the only other child on the Vineyard that I saw who was disabled. She developed a tumor on her spinal cord at an early age, and it caused her legs to be weak. She had an ataxic gait (difficulty keeping her balance), but she could still play tennis. I will talk later of disabled persons whom I personally know who have become professionals, mostly physicians.

As a child, I found many African American role models at the Vineyard. These professionals were regular visitors and many physicians. They played tennis at the annual Oak Bluff's Tennis Tournament during the Labor Day weekend. I continue to be inspired by disabled physicians who do not have time to focus on their difficulties but rather spend their lives caring for others.

Mom would introduce all of the doctors and their specialties. I learned about ophthalmologists, otolaryngologists, and cardiologists. Friends of the family in the medical professional circle included Dr. Benny Prim, Dr. Bill Hayling and his brother, Dr. Les Hayling, and Dr. Theodore Stent. Early on, I truly thought that all black boys grew up to become doctors. That is the power of role models.

My dream was to marry a pretty girl, have a family, become a doctor, and vacation on Martha's Vineyard every summer. I graduated from Meharry Medical College, became a board-certified medical doctor, married a pretty girl named Gloria, and at the age of forty-six, for the first time, with my family by my side, drove my late-model Jaguar to Martha's Vineyard. The story of my life is that dreams come true—for real.

My childhood friend, Dee Dee, is now an attorney. She functions independently with a wheelchair and is employed by Wal-Mart in Arkansas. Many of the children I met when I was growing up are doing well. Les Hayling Jr. is a dentist who provides dental services at the State of New Jersey Penitentiary. Bobby Cunningham followed in his mother's footsteps and became an ophthalmologist. Dr. Theodore Stent's two daughters, Michelle and Nicole, are both attorneys in New York. Each of these people will also attest to the significance of growing up with so many African American doctors, lawyers, and dentists in their lives.

In this world of doctors and lawyers, one needs a bit of humor. Leroy Banks, a real estate broker, is one of the funniest guys I've ever met, because he tells jokes and is in a good mood. When we see each other, we always say affectionately, "Here comes trouble." On the Vineyard, we have so much fun together. We share a lot of ageless insider jokes that have continued to bring smiles into our hearts and tears of joy to our eyes for four or more decades. Leroy is also known for his ability to give wise counsel, and I am told that he is a decent golfer.

I think spending summers on Martha's Vineyard while I was growing up was crucial. When I returned home and went back to school, I studied harder. The image of those doctors was fresh in my mind. One person on the Vineyard who stood out is Dr. Bill Hayling, obstetrician gynecologist. Even now, I have never seen him wear professional attire. He was always a walking definition of class. As the expression goes, Dr. Hayling was a "man among men." Other kids had athletes as role models, but I had Dr. Hayling. All year long, I would wait for the Labor Day weekend so I could see him. It was the way he walked, talked, dressed, and interacted with others. I thought he conducted himself the way that I, as a man, would someday.

Of course my father was an excellent role model, too. But I saw him just about every day. You tend to see your parents as parents, but others that you see only once a year and only in the same setting have a powerful effect on you.

When I later went to the Vineyard as a college student and a medical student, I had a much more mature understanding of the difficulties of acquiring that lifestyle. I knew I could not become a doctor only to live out childhood fantasies. Becoming a doctor was about patient care. There were political and social problems on the Vineyard that affected African Americans. I saw how difficult it was to buy property and the sacrifices involved in owning a second home. Gloria and I still go there each year around Labor Day, and so do a lot of my friends from the 1970s and 1980s.

I recall, as a young boy, I first met Bobby Cunningham, who is an ophthalmologist, and Les Hayling Jr., who is a dentist, while watching them play tennis at the Oak Bluffs Tennis Tournament each Labor Day weekend. I met Michelle and Nicole Stent on the beach at Martha's Vineyard while I was in grade school. Nicole is one of my sister's best friends to this day. Both Michelle and Nicole are attorneys in New York City. I have been in contact with these individuals for the past forty years. However, I haven't seen Dee Dee and still others in many years.

Each year, I continue to see fewer and fewer of my childhood mentors in human form, but they will continue to be with me in spirit, always. Many of them have joined my father, who went home to be with the Lord thirteen years ago. After all is said and done, I owe a great deal of gratitude to the the Vineyard connections and to my parents for introducing me to the island and all of my mentors. I am grateful to have been introduced to the black elite at such a young age.

It is important that children be exposed to positive role models during their formative years.

<u>Martha's Vineyard</u>

Wanda Williams, Cheryl,
Victor, Darrell, 1962

Dad, Cheryl, 1967

Bob Shaw, Quentin Vaughn, Darrell, 1972

Martha's Vineyard

CJ, Karen Spears, Gloria, Darrell, Les Hayling, Rupert,2006

Barry, Gloria, Carol, 1992

Darrell, Leroy Banks, 2006

KEY # 5: The physical, mental, and spiritual environment in which you spend most of your time is your life incubator. Examine your environment. Anyone or anything that does not support your dreams should be kept at arm's length.

* Be on the lookout for positive role models.
* Seek out people who have goals and dreams similar to yours.
* Identify and discuss your goals and dreams with people who have already gone where you want to go.
* Limit your involvement with people who talk negatively about you or your goals.

SUCCESS KEY #6

People Are Valuable Resources. Use Them Wisely.

THE HOLY ENCOUNTER

When you meet anyone, remember it is a holy
encounter. As you see him, you will see yourself. As
you treat him, you will treat yourself. As you think of
him, you will think of yourself. Never forget this, for
in him you will find yourself or lose yourself.
—from Marianne Williamson's *Return To Love*, 1992

Girls and Women

The very first girl I liked in grade school was Lolinda Lewis. She
lived down Cross Street from us. She was, by a consensus of the
community, the prettiest girl in our town. She was the girl who set the
standard of beauty, and a lot of boys liked her. I liked her because she
was extremely nice to me, much nicer than the others were. She never
made fun of me and often stood up for me when the other kids teased
me. She was older than the rest of us. Lolinda went to Fisk University
and relocated to Texas, where she became a schoolteacher. I saw her
when she came back to Long Island in 1988. She was just as attractive
as I remembered her from my childhood.

You may wonder what dating was like for me in high school and
other stages of my life. First of all, I never had a girlfriend in high
school. I was friends with everyone, boys and girls, and when this
happens you are not really close to anyone. I had low self-esteem, and
I would try to make up for this by trying to get a real pretty girlfriend
to pay me some attention. My rationale was that a pretty girlfriend
would somehow compensate for my disability. Teenage boys usually
like girls, and I was no exception.

In high school, I was a friend to a lot of the girls, but I never went steady with a girl. Girls were reluctant to dance with me at parties, especially slow dancing. Immediately after girls turned me down, they would dance with another guy who asked them to dance. This made me feel so bad. I felt that the girls did not want to dance with me because I was handicapped. If girls wouldn't dance with me, I didn't have a chance to get to know them because the music was too loud, so it was difficult for them to understand me when I spoke.

In college I fared better. The girls danced with me to fast and slow music. But I still couldn't find a steady girlfriend. For example, during my junior year, I really liked a girl who was a social work major. She knew I had strong feelings toward her, but she shared with me that her friends questioned why she would go out with me at all because I was disabled. In the end, she wanted to be "friends." In my senior year, I had a lab partner in one of my classes who knew I liked her a lot, but she also gave me the notorious "friends" line. In both instances, we went out on dates for a whole semester, and they dated other guys while dating me.

Once, I asked a girl to dance, but she thought I was drunk because of the way I walked and quickly turned away from me. On more than one occasion, a girl would make a date with me on a Monday and then break the date on Friday or Saturday. This hurt the most. I would anticipate going out with this particular girl all week, and then the big letdown would come on the evening of the date.

In the 1970s in Westbury, a guy had to dress well, smell good, drive his parents' nice car, be a good student, and, of course, be good-looking. In the African American community, it was expected that guys would also be great basketball players. You *had* to play well. The guys always looked up to the city guys and tried to emulate their game and wear the same type of sneakers they wore. The most popular were suede sneakers with contrasting laces.

One of our biggest role models was Frankie Crocker, a New York disc jockey who hosted a show on the radio station WBLS. He was really cool on the air. He had a deep, smooth voice and dressed in a real cool style. Frankie often hosted jam sessions throughout the five boroughs of New York City and could be seen on flyers and the sides of buses. He was the number one DJ in his time slot for more than thirty years. When we heard "Moody's Mood for Love," by Eddie

Jefferson, we knew it was 8 PM, because that was the song Frankie signed on with for all of those years. The girls loved the Chief Rocker, as he called himself. I would try to rap to the girls like Frankie did, but I simply was not Frankie, so I wasn't very successful using his lines.

On a high school trip to an amusement park, I tried to put into action what I had learned from my most admired radio personality and my friends. I thought that I would be successful, but I was not sure how it would work out. Nevertheless, I started rapping to a certain girl I liked. When I began talking, she rejected me and talked to my friend. I guess she had trouble understanding me because of my disability, even though I tried the same lines my buddies used. My difficulty with clear articulation made it impossible to convince her that I was the best guy for her.

While participating in the Jack and Jill organization, a social organization for middle-class blacks in which children could meet and socialize with other middle-class black kids, I experienced some of my biggest childhood disasters in practicing the fine art of rapping while attempting to learn how to play the dating game. Each month, the parents would plan an activity for the children to attend—usually on Saturday afternoons. In high school there were a lot of dances, but the big dance was held at Christmas. The thought behind Jack and Jill was that children could make lasting friendships with other children within the organization. It was not uncommon for a boy and a girl to grow up in Jack and Jill and become husband and wife as adults.

For me, Jack and Jill was a nightmare. My mother signed me up when I was a small child, and I stayed in it through high school. The girls were very cruel to me. They made fun of me and rarely went out with me. I simply didn't pass the test for acceptance. They seemed to want to date the guys who were more athletic or the guys who were from New York City or the guys who wore leather jackets. Some of the preferred specimens were more like young men than the gentler, erudite boys of Long Island.

As a member of the Jack and Jill organization, I didn't realize that girls were not interested in someone who had CP. Many within the group didn't understand my condition, because it was not something that was talked about openly. Dating was problematic for me because I could not meet the girls' expectations of how a boyfriend was supposed to look and act. The girls were condescending and patronizing most of the time. Sometimes I could get them to dance with me. I did not get their phone numbers. I was not taken seriously as a potential boyfriend. I became frustrated. Frustration and a lot of self-pity set in, and they contributed to my feelings of low self-esteem. However, close friends who are current members of the group say that the organization has grown tremendously since the 1960s and 1970s when I was involved.

I did have some dating success in the eleventh grade. I took Poncheta Pope, a very lovely girl, to the junior prom, and we looked great together. We were dressed in our best for the occasion. It was one of the most wonderful days of my life. I could not contain the laughter in my heart. I will always remember my beautiful date and all of the details of my junior prom. That was a very big score for me. Smile! Smile! Smile! This was a big boost to my self-confidence. Although we lost contact after high school, I will always remember her.

I was not a nerd. I knew the latest dances, the top celebrities, and the coolest music, and I wore the trendy clothes. I was hip to the happenings. One strategy I used was to let the girls see me talking to the athletes and the more desirable guys, thinking this would help me get a date, or at least a phone number. But that did not work either. The girls who would talk to me would say, "Darrell, let's just be friends." But I already had lots of platonic girlfriends. I was good-looking, or so they would say, and very popular, yet I was not sought after. I allowed the girls to define my sense of self-worth. That can be extremely dangerous and can produce some disastrous results. My mom and dad advised me against chasing girls, and they were right.

In high school, in college, and as a practicing physician, I made mistakes while playing the dating game. My father told me time and time again throughout my dating life, "Talk to the girls who are interested in you." This was very sound advice, but I was not willing to receive it until many years later. I think it was a mistake for me not to discuss my CP with the girls when we were in school or on a date. It may have made a positive difference in our relationship. I finally corrected this mistake when I dated in my thirties. I took the time to explain the nature of my disability to women in whom I had an interest, and I was told by many of my dates that this was very helpful.

I'd had eyes on Janice Ferebee since the fifth grade, and she had been a cheerleader in high school. After my freshman year in college we went to the beach together, and I felt so proud to be with her.

At Howard University, I was well-known, and there were lots of parties and discos every week. I made the mistake of going to discos. That was a bad experience for two reasons. First, the music was so loud. It was difficult for me to have any conversation, because my speech was slurred and my voice was quiet. Second, the girls may have thought that I was drunk because of the way I walked and talked. I should have found other places to socialize, such as museums, book clubs, and art shows. Although I wasn't always a good dancer, because it was a challenge to keep to the beat, the girls would still dance with me.

My social life was somewhat challenging. In 1985, during my fellowship training at Harlem Hospital, I met a nursing student named Janice Howard who was very nice. She was warm, understanding, and attractive. We dated almost every weekend. I wined her and dined her to the hilt. We had dinner at Windows of the World, a restaurant at the top of the World Trade Center. We enjoyed each other's company, and together we shared many fun-filled dates, but that was as far as it went.

In September 1989 I attended the Congressional Black Caucus Meeting in Washington DC, and I met an interesting woman. I could do no wrong in her eyes. Shortly thereafter, she began to be critical of the way I ate with my mouth open, which of course was due to my CP. I tried to explain that to her. Then she was very critical of the Christmas presents that I gave her. In three months she went from being crazy about me to being overly critical of me. During a New Year's brunch, that relationship ended. Based on my dad's advice for successful dating, I thought I had chosen the right woman this time. Parting was bitter and sweet. Needless to say, I was disappointed. From playing the dating game, I learned that you have to play in order to win; play is not always fair, and a father's advice, even if it isn't always right, is priceless.

I remember once during my residency, an inpatient, about my age, suffering from rheumatoid arthritis at Harlem Hospital had a crush on me. This is a common occurrence with doctors and patients. Her fingers had become deviated, which means that they were curved toward the pinkie because of the arthritis. In medicine, this is called *ulnar deviation*. The patient would frequently ask the nurse to send for me for minor complaints just to have me see her. When I walked into her room, her eyes would light up, and she would smile. I was about six months into my fellowship, so I was very inexperienced at handling this situation. I should have consulted with the senior physicians, but I didn't. I was flattered. I thought her affection was either because I was good-looking or because I was a doctor.

Nothing serious developed, because I stayed out of harm's way. I knew it was not a good idea for doctors to become romantically involved with patients. It was probably illegal and definitely improper medical ethics. I also knew that in my career, I would probably encounter this again, and I would have to gain experience in how to handle it. Now, I just tell patients that I'm married. I even have a picture of my wife on my desk.

We were taught during our residency training that the disabled are often taken advantage of socially and sexually. In other words, the nondisabled will date the disabled for sexual satisfaction and then drop them like a broken toy. I have never personally experienced this, but the residents discussed it, and numerous medical textbooks discuss this problem.

Like many of my male friends, I was most interested in women because of their looks. But, for me, dating posed still another problem. When I went to social events with females, I had to be the one to get the drinks, as this was customary behavior for the man. Early on, I had been taught proper dating manners. On a date, it was very important to me to do things according to what I knew to be correct and proper. I had difficulty carrying a drink from the bar to our table without spilling it. This was not because my hands were unsteady but because my gait was ataxic, which means that I had an uncoordinated base of support when I walked. To prevent spillage, I would sometimes ask my date or someone else to carry the drinks for me. This always embarrassed me and made me feel as if my date couldn't count on me to be "the man."

When I attended medical conferences and cocktail receptions later in life, we are expected to stand and engage in small talk while trying to balance food and drink. This is a problem for me. So, I try to just have finger foods and nonalcoholic beer or, better yet, find someplace to sit down. At conferences, when coffee was served, I came up with the idea of pouring half a cup into another cup. Then I can make two trips to the table without spilling, or I can stand and drink the half-cup of coffee.

Kissing and intimacy also posed a problem while I was dating. It was very embarrassing to drool while kissing or engaging in pillow talk. In relationships, communication is so important. I could not find the place or time to talk about CP with a woman I was dating. This was definitely a costly mistake on my part. By not talking about it, I was not able to develop closer relationships with them. After all, I was a physician and should have been able to discuss illnesses easily.

These experiences were the building blocks that prepared me for the most important relationship of my life, marriage.

My Wife

In 1991 I met a wonderful woman at Martha's Vineyard by the name of Gloria Nixon, who later became my wife. I had prayed for a loving, caring woman to be by my side, and my prayers were answered. Meeting Gloria was much like a fantasy. Many may dream of going on vacation and meeting a beautiful woman on the beach. For me, this really happened.

Gloria saw how I walked, because I was wearing shorts. My walking did not seem to bother her at all. She challenged me to a chess game at the Ink Well. We played, she won, we played again, and the rest is history. I am fortunate to have met someone who loves the game of chess as much as I do.

I did not see Gloria again for a few years. Perhaps the timing was not right for us then. Chess and our social time together took a backseat to other areas of our lives. In any event, we drifted apart. During that time, Gloria continued with her volunteerism, began working on a master's of divinity degree, and traveled abroad. I was very busy studying to pass boards for medical certification while working. Personal visits and all phone communications had stopped completely.

But in 1996 Gloria found my old business card with my home number written on the back; she called me for a game of chess, and we did play some chess. We also went out to the first of many dinners. The local newspaper had printed a list of all of the restaurants on Long Island that were located on the water. Gloria and I both enjoy fine dining with the added benefits of a wonderful oceanic view. We went on dates each weekend for about two years. I took her to many waterfront restaurants, and we fell in love. By 1999, we knew we wanted to get married and became officially engaged in January 2000.

Gloria is from Arkansas. She is one of eight children. She has five brothers: Lee Amos, Sherman, Lee Chester, Iziah Jr., and Jerrell. Her sisters are Daisy Mae and Lar. Joe, Lar's husband, and Lar are counted among our closest friends.

Gloria's mother, Mrs. Ardella Nixon, wanted a dainty little girl. This was her hope and her prayer. Her first child was a boy, Lee Amos. Then she gave birth to Sherman and Lee Chester. With three boys to her credit, she held her desire of mothering a little girl close to her heart and firmly in her prayers. God granted her the desire of her heart.

When Gloria was born, her mom shouted, "This is glorious!" For Gloria's mom, this was a dream come true and a long-awaited answer to her prayer. Now she had a girl whom she could dress with ribbons in her hair. Mrs. Nixon wanted to give the name Glorious to the newest member of the family. But Aunt Lula, mother Nixon's older sister, convinced her to name the newborn Gloria.

Gloria liked to climb trees as a child. She describes herself as a tomboy growing up. She loved to wrestle with her brothers, too, and later learned to play chess with them. Chess was considered a boys' game, and she could only play if she was competitive. So she improved her skills by challenging players she knew could beat her at the game. Later, she took chess lessons from a grand master, and this built her confidence as a talented player.

Soon after high school, Gloria moved to Queens, found work, and went to college. While working in the banking industry, her talents as a leader were recognized, and the bank sent her to college and paid for it in full. She obtained a degree in computer information systems in 1981. After earning her degree, she went from being a vice president at a major bank on Wall Street to becoming an entrepreneur who owned her own real estate company called Glorious New Homes Realty. She also hosted her own public access television show called

Inside Real Estate with Gloria Nixon. Her dream was to end homelessness in New York City and to show African Americans how they could own a home instead of renting. But the competitive business of real estate was not fulfilling as she had hoped, so she decided to study ministry.

I had prayed so hard for God to bring me a wife. I had many struggles trying to find a nice girlfriend, and God blessed me with Gloria Jean. Gloria and I were married June 23, 2001, and God blessed us with a beautiful day full of sunshine.

We made it through the long courtship, more than a thousand chess games of winning ... and losing. Gloria had her sister Lar, my sister Cheryl, as well as some of the bridesmaids assist her in getting dressed in her home in Queens, New York. The photographer began working early that morning, putting this with that and moving this person near that person and shooting lots of pictures. Gloria told me it was uncomfortable having so many people poking at her all morning.

When it was time, I began to get dressed with the help of my very best man—my big brother, Victor. After I put on my tuxedo, Victor drove me to the church in my Jaguar. I kept thinking, "Here I am, finally getting married at forty-six years old."

Vic and I were in the room behind the church pulpit where our choir stores their robes. I must admit I was a bit nervous, but Vic joked with me to get me to feel more relaxed, and I did. I kept telling myself that weddings are mostly for the bride and that I, as the groom, was just there to help Gloria on *her* day.

As I watched my future wife approach the altar, I marveled at how beautiful she looked. She walked slowly, carrying her flowers. Gloria had done so much for so many, and today was her day to be pampered. With the woman I loved, whom God had given me, slowly approaching me at the altar, I could hardly contain myself. But I did.

In addition to "the guys," the wedding party consisted of the maid of honor, Lar Watkins, and four bridesmaids, Dr. Alma Norment Martin, Kathy Pittman, Delphine Smith, and Lauren Outlaw. My niece Sarah Grace was the flower girl. Mrs. Denise Luther Williams coordinated the rehearsal and wedding at the church, and Lar coordinated all other aspects leading up to our big day. Both did splendid jobs. Every detail was perfectly implemented.

Pastor Duggan presided over the ceremony in a white African robe with rich embroidery on the sleeves, which was very sharp and perfect for this most glorious event in my life. As the pastor faced the congregation with my family to his left and Gloria's family to his right, he read from the United Church of Christ's book of worship, and then he asked our families to stand. Then he asked, "Do you promise your love and support to Darrell and Gloria? If so, please say, 'I do with the help of God.'"

The ceremony was wonderful. We exchanged our wedding vows, took Communion, and affirmed our love for each other. Then the pastor said, "You may kiss the bride." Several of the witnesses said that our ceremonial kiss could have been nominated to the *Guinness Book of Records* as the longest kiss ever! We jumped the broom, which is an African tradition symbolizing the start of a new life together, greeted our guests, and went to the reception at the Chateau Briand in our white limo. Howard Tate, our videographer, was well-known for his work for network television at the Olympics. He was a blessing.

Our first dance was to Céline Dion's "Because You Loved Me." We later did the electric slide. We also had live entertainment and an energetic DJ who got the guests on the dance floor. It was a perfect wedding day that we will never forget. Before that day, I used to cry in my car after church because I didn't have a wife or a girlfriend to love or to love me.

My wife has a master's degree in professional studies and a master's of divinity from New York Theological Seminary. She earned her doctorate in theological studies in May 2004. Gloria now serves as associate pastor of the Congregational Church of South Hempstead, where we both participate in ministry.

My wife is very loving, sweet, warm, and intelligent. I take her out on a date every week. Fine dining, jazz, and dancing are gourmet foods for the soul. I also enjoy dancing with her in the kitchen to the sound of *The Simpsons Sing the Blues*, especially track seven, titled "I Love to See You Smile." For those of you who are in a special relationship, I highly recommend dancing in the kitchen with your sweetie. It might not have any therapeutic value, and then again, it might. In any event, it may prove to be a different kind of fun thing to do. Just try it.

Gloria and I have a lot in common. We still travel to Martha's Vineyard; she comes with me to medical conferences because she is interested in health issues. We like to travel together. Gloria and I play a lot of chess. We have a golden crown that sits atop the head of the one who wins the most chess games that day. For a day, the champion is given royal extravagances and is treated in a manner that befits a king or queen. Sometimes, I am truly the king of our castle, and other times, well, I'm looking for the book *How to Beat Your Wife in Chess*.

She says that her strength is perseverance. She does not believe in giving up just because a thing is tough. She has a thorough knowledge of CP, because I have educated her about my condition. She has been very understanding and supportive, which means the world to me. The key in finding a spouse if you have a disability, I've found, is to be honest about the disability and let your potential spouse know all of the ramifications so he or she can make an informed decision to get involved or not.

<u>My Wife</u>

Alma, Lar, Kathy
Delphine, Gloria, Lauren

Alpha Phi Alpha Fraternity Inc.

I pledged Alpha in my second semester of my sophomore year at C. W. Post College. Usually premed students do not have time to pledge. I knew the history of Alpha men. We were founded in 1906. We were the first black fraternity in America, and a lot of African American men are Alphas. Alpha Phi Alpha has long stood at the forefront of the African American community's fight for civil rights through leaders such as W. E. B. DuBois, Adam Clayton Powell Jr., Edward Brooke, Martin Luther King Jr., Thurgood Marshall, Andrew Young, William Gray, Paul Robeson, Congressman Charles Rangel, and many others. I pledged because the fraternity emphasizes education and brotherly love.

I knew that being an Alpha and a physician would open great doors for me socially and politically, and it has. I have come across many great Alpha brothers in my journey through life. Among them are Matthew Woods, a dentist from college, and Michael Bertty, who works in conflict resolution. My brothers from Meharry are the following: Drs. Norman Jones, Bayne Spotwood, Leonard Little, Darrell Robinson, Jay Randall Byrd, and Audley Mackel. We do a great deal of community work.

THEN
(1906)

NOW
(2006)

KEY # 6: Often we think of resources as things, but people are resources too. And, whether you know it or not, there are many people who are willing and able to help you reach your goals. When you meet these people who have been selected to be a part of your destiny, treat them with respect.

* During the initial stages of relationships, nurture the ones that you consider valuable. They will usually grow into strong networking or support group opportunities.
* Identify the unique strengths of your friends and encourage them to develop these traits, as this can lead to lifelong friendships.
* Do not hesitate to take part-time jobs. They can help you develop skills, both technical and interpersonal, that will be useful in your profession.
* Choose wisely the people with whom you share personal information. It should be shared on a need-to-know basis. In my case, telling my date about my disability and the things I have learned to compensate for would have helped her make more informed choices. Your spouse is your soul mate.
* Find a hobby/ game that you can enjoy with your spouse, as this is a diversion from the everyday stresses.
* Develop a sense of humor. Be able to laugh at yourself as well as others.
* Make sure that the relationship is reciprocal. Even if you have disabilities, there are lots of things you can do to make the other person feel appreciated.

SUCCESS KEY #7

Develop a Plan or Borrow One from a Role Model. Then Set Goals and Attain Them.

Plans go wrong for lack of advice; many counselors bring success.
— *Proverbs 15:22*

Get all the advice and instruction you can, and be wise
the rest of your life.
— *Proverbs 19:20*

Mentors

Every successful person I know or have heard about has mentors and role models. These are the people who show us how to map out our lives in a manner that helps us get the job done. These leaders are the ones who help us to navigate our way through life obstacles to success. In any profession, you need mentors. I want to discuss three of the doctors who are responsible for my being the doctor that I am today. They are Dr. Lawrence Friedman, Dr. Herbert Thornhill, and Dr. Jerry Weissman. These doctors were very important in my development as an individual and to the maturation of my skills and practice as a doctor.

The late Dr. Lawrence Friedman was chairman of the Department of Physical Medicine and Rehabilitation at Nassau County Medical Center, where I did my residency. Dr. Friedman was hard on his residents and demanded a lot of them. I was with him from 1981 to 1984. He once told me that his experience with people with CP was that they are lazy. I couldn't believe he said that. The whole world was applauding my accomplishments. I had just graduated from medical school two months prior. Instead of recognizing that, he just told me to not be lazy. He was Dad's age and had almost twenty years of experience in rehabilitation medicine. In spite of what he said, he hired me. Obviously, he thought I had some potential.

He was strict. Tardiness, for example, was completely unacceptable for residents. Rounds began at 8:00, not 8:05. When he asked a question during rounds, he would stare at the resident and never crack a smile. We made rounds with therapists, social workers, and nurses. If one of his doctors didn't know an answer, he would ask a physical therapist instead and purposely make the doctor feel bad. This was done, actually, to encourage us to read more.

Dr. Friedman was an early riser. His lectures started promptly at the appointed time. If there was just one resident present out of ten, he would start. He knew that my hands were spastic, but he demanded that I button the top button of my shirt and, of course, wear my tie.

The highest praise he ever gave me was during morning rounds. I had all the necessary instruments he needed to remove a bandage from a patient's stump after leg amputation, and he liked that I was fully prepared and the other two physicians were not. *Stump* is the anatomical term for that part of the leg that remains after the leg has been amputated.

He was probably the world's leading authority on lower extremity amputation and prescribing prosthesis. He lectured all over the world. He wanted us to be experts in that area of rehabilitation. In America, the number one cause of amputation, nontraumatic, is diabetes mellitus. In such cases, much important information is gathered about the amputated foot by closely examining the foot on the leg that is still in place. Dr. Friedman always said, "Examine the other foot first!"

Many people say I inspire them because I became a doctor. But Dr. Friedman motivated me to push further and further. He always told me that I had to be twice as good as anyone else because I was black and disabled. I am so blessed to have had Dr. Freidman as my chairman. God placed him in my life at the right time.

One day at a medical conference in Los Angeles, Dr. Friedman introduced me to Dr. Herbert Louis Thornhill (Dr. T.), one of his classmates from Howard University's medical school. I was honored. He was the first African American physiatrist I had ever met. Later that evening, Dr. T. and I sat in a sports bar and watched Monday Night Football. During the first half, he told me he was the Director of Rehabilitation Medicine at Harlem Hospital and said there was a position open for a fellowship after I graduated residency. I had a formal interview when we returned to New York. I accepted his offer and began my fellowship on July 1, 1984.

Dr. Thornhill was the opposite of Dr. Friedman. He was really impressed that an African American male with CP had become a doctor and had chosen his specialty. Dr. T. had previously worked with a physician who was disabled, Dr. Albert Anderson, past Chairman of Rehabilitation at Harlem Hospital and a sufferer of Lou Gehrig's disease. Dr. Anderson was wheelchair-bound with a respirator attached to the back of his chair.

Tardiness was not a big deal with Dr. T. If the tie was not straight or the top button not buttoned, you didn't have to worry about it. He was laid-back, but he was also extremely sensitive to the issues of poor, disabled people. His patient population was predominately amputees and patients who suffered from strokes.

Dr. T. led rounds that were so insightful. He suggested, for example, that diabetes-induced poor vision could explain why patients couldn't put on their prostheses. He got me involved in a research project evaluating blind amputees. I regret that I did not finish the project and publish it in a medical journal. He spent more than twenty years treating poor and disabled elderly people.

Almost all his patients had diabetes mellitus, hypertension, heart disease, or kidney disease. Harlem Hospital has an Independent Living Center for the disabled. Some of Dr. Thornhill's patients with amputated feet ran successfully in the New York City Marathon every fall.

Dr. Thornhill was honored a few years ago in New York City for his many years of service to the disabled population. I attended the ceremony, and there I gained a deeper understanding of his commitment to his work. I kept the home address and the phone number that Dr. T. had given me years ago, and I used it to send him an invitation to our wedding. I was delighted that he accepted. He and his wife, Martha, witnessed our marriage vows.

One night at a medical conference, I was speaking to a physiatrist who needed some part-time, temporary help. His name is Dr. Jerry

Weissman (Dr. JW), and he was the Director of Rehabilitation Medicine at Elmhurst Hospital in Elmhurst, Queens. That temporary job lasted nine years and culminated when I passed the Rehabilitation Boards. My title was Assistant Attending Physician. Dr. Weissman is a walking textbook. He knows everything about rehab medicine.

Residents usually try to avoid conferences, but they never miss his conferences. I've learned more in one hour with him than in three hours of reading a textbook. The first day at work, he told me to teach the residents. I was really happy with that, because I love to teach. Both Dr. JW and Dr. T. displayed a very high level of interest in patients' care, and they exhibited a genuine concern for residents as well. Dr. T. was systematic in his teaching. Under his care, I learn so much new material. He even made the Journals Club interesting. During the Journals Club, a resident has to discuss in detail an article in one of the medical journals.

Dr. Weissman allowed me to give formal lectures to his residents. I lectured on shoulder pain. Working with Dr. Weissman was great because the residents were just out of medical school. They were usually between the ages of twenty-six and thirty. They were bright and willing to learn. These doctors-to-be were being prepared for the boards that they would have to pass before becoming certified. Because of my work with the residents, I was cited as being one of the best teachers in our department. At Elmhurst Hospital, I learned how to teach from the expert, Dr. Weissman.

From 1992 to 1997, I worked in the back clinic, which was the most dreaded clinic in the department. There were two lovely ladies who worked with me. They were the best. Their names are Diana Jean and Ann Marie. They were very helpful to me. They called themselves, collectively, the Ponettes. Dr. Weissman gave me the approval to bring a baby doll to the clinic to facilitate the education of the patients about their back pain and proper care. Initially, I don't think Dr. Friedman would have allowed me to play with dolls while earning a doctor's salary. He could have said no dolls and insisted on other methods of sharing information with the patients. But he said yes. To this day, when I teach, I use dolls to facilitate the learning process.

We named this little stuffed doll "the pink thing" because of its color. I drew a diagram of a pinched nerve on the doll's body to review low-back anatomy. The patients enjoyed learning, and they became totally invested in the healing process. I have taught individual patients, families, and groups. I have reviewed neck, back, shoulder, and knee pain, as well as the diabetic foot. The talks are always well received. Dr. Weissman understood the importance of arming every person with medical knowledge. He is devoted to learning and teaching others.

Of course, you can imagine all the jokes I heard about having a doll with me at work. I told patients that I worked in the back clinic because it was the only job I could find that would allow me to bring my doll to work. One December, Diana jokingly said she was going to buy me a doll for Christmas.

Much like Dr. Weissman, my staff and I have developed an insatiable desire to share what we have learned from others. I love to teach. I teach health topics at career day assemblies in public schools, at churches, and at social and political gatherings. I teach other doctors and students of all ages. I am eager to speak in classrooms in our community. My pay, which is more than sufficient, is usually a thank-you note or a generous plaque. However, when a large brown envelope from the Park Avenue Elementary School, where I had recently participated in the Community Career Day, arrived in the mail, I was more than just curious. In it was a book of thank-you letters[ii] from Mrs. Sill's first-grade class. Seeing the artwork and reading the beautifully crafted words of thanks from a group of children, some of whom may become doctors, is rewarding. I am from a school of thought that compels me to be an active participant in the mentoring of others.

I also had relatives who were crucial in my development: Uncle Johnny, Uncle Julian, and Aunt Betty. I first met Uncle Johnny when I was in grade school. Uncle Johnny and Aunt Eleanor, my father's sister, were married at our home when I was five years old. He always supported me in my studies. He knew that I could become a doctor. He was my dad's best friend, even though he lived in Trenton, New Jersey. He constantly told me to study hard. Uncle Johnny was a good ole country boy from North Carolina. When I was a child, he taught me how to work hard physically. We would do all of the chores at his house or mine whenever we visited. He was a blue-collar worker with a good work ethic. He reminded me of Dr. Friedman. He gave me great counsel about medical school and told me to balance my studies with social activities.

Uncle Julian, in contrast, was all about fun. He was a police officer in Philadelphia. He was one of the few adults who actually played a little rough with me when I was a kid, and I loved it. He is tall and well built. It was fun being around him. I used to spend a weekend with him every year until I got married. He was at my graduation from medical school and at my wedding.

Aunt Betty is my godmother. She used to take care of my brother and sister and I when my parents went on vacation. Not everyone is blessed to have a godmother like I am. Aunt Betty took me to therapy when my parents were on vacation. She was a guidance counselor on Long Island, so she also gave me wise counsel about education when I was in school. She gave me insightful information about passing the SATs, and she helped me to choose the right college. Whenever we had parties at our house and folks needed someplace to stay overnight, she would always open her home. She and my mother are like sisters. Both she and her husband, Attah-Jundwe, have been our close family friends for decades now.

The importance of my mentors is that they showed me the way. They were able to put me on the right path. In today's world it is very important to know right from wrong. The world is so complex that it is sometimes not always easy to make that distinction.

> Obey your leaders and submit to their authority. They keep
> watch over you as men who must give an account.
> Obey them so that their work will be a joy, not a burden,
> for that would be of no advantage to you.
> — *Hebrews 13:17 (NIV)*

<u>Mentors</u>

Aunt Betty

Frankie
Crocker,
WBLS-FM

Dr.& Mrs. Manderville &
Mom

Uncle Johnny

Uncle Julian

It's Great Being a Doctor!

There are so many advantages to being a medical doctor. I enjoy the practice of physiatry because rehabilitation medicine allows me to help people become more functional.

I treat patients with low-back pain. Low-back pain is the number one reason people miss work. There are a variety of causes for low-back pain, but much of my treatment consists of injecting the patient with a local anesthetic plus a small amount of steroids in the lower back area. Patients get immediate relief that can last two to four weeks. They are amazed with the results after a period of treatment. My spastic hands do not prevent me from giving injections—thank God for that.

I love to educate patients about the proper way to sit, stand, and drive a car in the presence of low-back pain. When they return to my office to let me know how these suggestions have worked, I feel great. I once had a barber who suffered from low-back pain. I suggested that he put his foot on a stool when he's standing and working in order to relieve the stress on his back, and it worked. His praise of me did not go unnoticed.

I customize the treatment for each patient. Dr. Friedmann taught me how to do that during my residency. I also learned how to maintain a high level of patient dignity, care, and courtesy. In medical school, one of our professors repeatedly reminded us to treat the patient as well as the disease. He would say, "It is not only what disease the patient has, but rather the patient who has the disease." In other words, patient care and patient cure go hand in hand. This is extremely important in rehabilitation medicine. For example, low-back pain in a lawyer is different from low-back pain in a construction worker and would be managed differently. The treatment plan for back pain in a pregnant woman differs greatly from that of a nonpregnant woman.

I have worked with young mothers with low-back pain. I keep a doll in the office to show them the proper way to feed, cuddle, bathe, dress, and lift. Of course the infants are larger and heavier than the doll, but it gives them some guidelines. I also have models of the lumbar and cervical spine as well as a knee model.

When my wife and I attended a medical conference, I ran into some of my former residents, and they told me how much they appreciated my teaching from years ago. I enjoy getting involved in the academic discussions at conferences. There I can appreciate the art and science of medicine. The exchange of ideas with other doctors is great. We also attend the journal club, where the latest journals help us to build on our knowledge, and the discussions led by several physicians help us to think more analytically. We also discuss patients' illnesses and ways to better our patient management. Fortunately, in these conferences, my disability is a nonissue. We are all focused on the topics.

Every year I attend conferences sponsored by the NMA. It is always helpful to learn the latest medical advances, to exchange ideas with other doctors, and to see old friends from all over the country. Being a doctor has provided me a most enjoyable career in service to humanity. The opportunity to travel to the Caribbean and to several cities throughout the country is a wonderful side benefit.

The NMA is composed of predominately African American physicians. I have been a member of the NMA since I started my career and have met some dynamic doctors. We work hard in our varied practices to eliminate health-care disparities in African American patients. Dr. Winston Price, president of the NMA, is a leader in medical computer technology. Dr. Price is a pediatrician.

Dr. Carol Britton is an attending physician at Columbia University School of Medicine in New York City. She is a neurologist. Dr. Britton organizes the NMA's offshore conferences. In addition to being a leader in the field of neurology, she is a skilled organizer. The organizing co-chairperson of the NMA is my good friend Dr. Jay Cowan. Dr. Cowan is a gastroenterologist in New York City, and his wife is Susan.

Some of these medical professionals are newcomers to the organization, and others, like me, had parents who were members of the NMA. As second-generation members, I and a few others have been active participants for two or more decades. Both Dr. Rachel Villaneuva, who practices medicine at New York University, and Dr.

M. Natlie Achong, who practices at Yale, are obstetricians and members of the NMA.

Dr. Kevin Means and Dr. Lisa Merritt are with the NMA, and they are also physiatrists. As a child, I never imagined that African American physicians would become experts on CP. I knew Dr. Merritt and Dr. Means as a child, and of course they never made fun of my disability. I've known Dr. Albright since 1977, and he is dedicated to continued education for doctors.

African American physicians comprise only 3 percent of all physicians. I am truly blessed to know so many. With all of the poor press African Americans receive, especially black men, I know a whole lot of doctors, and that is truly a blessing.

I also travel to medical conferences sponsored by the American Academy of Physical Medicine and Rehabilitation. There I see other physicians with disabilities. These disabilities include CP, blindness, amputated limbs, and spinal cord injuries. The former president of this organization is Dr. Thomas Strax. He also has CP, and he functions with the aid of a scooter. I met Dr. Strax during my residency and was in awe of him being a doctor. He was very helpful to me. He has difficulty speaking also, but I can understand him very well. Today he is a professor and chairman of the Department of Physical Medicine at the Robert Wood Johnson Medical School in Edison, New Jersey.

A woman with myotonic dystrophy (a form of muscle weakness) is the chairwoman of the Department of Physical Medicine and Rehabilitation. She was the past chairwoman at another hospital. I know a physiatrist who has a prosthesis on one of his arms. There are several doctors who have spinal cord injuries and practice medicine at the wheelchair level. When you see these doctors, you have to admire them. They all have made accomplishments in spite of their disabilities. In fact, when I look at them, I do not see disabilities but rather their tremendous abilities.

I presented a paper at the national meeting of the NMA in Atlanta. It was titled "Experiences of Being a Physiatrist with Cerebral Palsy." I gave the same lecture at Grand Rounds at Harlem Hospital and The Mount Sinai School of Medicine, both in New York City. The paper was well received at each event. I have never worked with another physically disabled physician, but we always share experiences at these conferences.

One of my most enjoyable experiences is talking to children during career day at the various schools in our community. I am known in education circles and asked to participate every year. Many of our young people want to be doctors.

I will never forget one boy in grade school who wanted to be a doctor. I asked him, "Who would you see first in the emergency room, pretty girls or an elderly patient who was equally as ill?" To my disappointment, he answered, "The pretty girls." I try to give the children an accurate picture of what it's like to be a doctor. I try to stay away from the area of CP. They enjoy listening to their heartbeats with the stethoscope, and sometimes they examine a doll. One of the children became saddened when she did not hear anything as she listened for the doll's heartbeat. I politely reminded her that it was a doll.

I drive a late-model Jaguar. It is my car of choice. This is not surprising, since many doctors drive them. The unique thing is how I purchased mine. One hot summer afternoon, I was wearing shorts. Whenever I do, it is obvious that I have a disability, because my left knee is slightly bent. As I was looking at the cars on the lot, the salesman came out to greet me. He didn't make the assumption that I could not afford a car due to my disability. We discussed the car, and when I told him I was a doctor, I received a great deal of respect from him. We went into the office, and he wrote up the sale. I found it amazing that he gave me more respect than a salesman at a men's clothing store. They continue to keep our apple red Jaguar running smooth.

I like to relate these experiences so the reader knows that there are wonderful people in the world who are warm and caring in the face of disability. I can say that the positive outweighs the negative. I realize that there is truly beauty in life, and we must recognize it. All of the hard work in school and in the practice paid dividends. There is so much joy in having friends in medicine and other professions.

Worship the Lord with gladness; come before him
with joyful songs.
— *Proverbs 100:2 (NIV)*

KEY # 7: According to the old saying, "When the pupil is ready, the teacher will appear." So, it is important to have a plan, a road map to your destination, and to start traveling down that road. Once you start toward your destination, people who have been there will suddenly appear in your life. Spend time with them and determine their strategies for success, how they overcame obstacles, and how they dealt with setbacks.

* You never know who will become your mentor, so keep an open mind.
* Find mentors, people who are willing to share the wisdom of their success with you, and embrace them.
* Understand that some mentors use tough love. Others are softer, but both are equally important.
* Your mentors will see in you what no one else sees.
* If a mentor is a celebrity, make sure that he or she can spend quality time with you.
* Mentors come in both genders with various racial identities, economic statuses, and ages.

SUCCESS KEY #8

Learn Your Craft Well and Stand Apart from the Crowd.

*Do not go where the path may lead, go instead
where there is no path and leave a trail.*
— *Ralph Waldo Emerson*

My biggest fear while working through medical school was gross anatomy. We called it "gross" for short. I dreaded trying to dissect a cadaver with my spastic hands. I was not afraid of the cadaver or the smell of formaldehyde—it was just the physical problems involved with dissection. One spastic move might cut a small nerve, artery, or vein, which then makes identifying the structure impossible.

The exam had two parts: the written and the practical. The written was taken from the lecture notes, and the practical was based on the student's ability to identify different structures on the cadaver. Fortunately, my anxiety never resulted in any problems. I loved working in the lab. I took the class during the summer between my freshman and sophomore years. It was my only class. It involved two or three hours of lectures in the morning and three to four hours of lab in the afternoon. My gross anatomy professor was Dr. Hines. She was very strict and demanded that her students be on time. She did not tolerate students entering her classroom after the scheduled beginning of class. If you were late for her lecture, you could not enter through the main door; you had to very quietly come in the back way.

In lab, we worked in teams. There were seven guys on our team. We had a lot of fun, but we helped each other learn a lot about anatomy. Benny Allison was the lead dissector. Benny is from Ohio and loved to dissect. One day I had an anatomy notebook with me, and on the front at the top I wrote the word *Gross* and then on the bottom I wrote my name, *Pone*. The problem was that it looked like *Gross Pone*. Yes, to this day Benny thinks my name is Gross Pone.

The team members I remember most are Benny, Jimmy, Will, and Ivan. Ivan Cozart was very studious. I remember Jimmy Cowan mostly because of his nickname, "Jimmy Mack." Will Gee was a very serious student. He is now practicing family medicine in Chicago.

One of the lab assistants was not pleased with me and complained that I was not doing enough dissection. I did what I could, given my God-given abilities and limitations. I think he was jealous of me because I had CP and still knew just as much as the rest of my classmates.

My favorite study partner who was not a lab partner was Lei Charlton, who is from Richmond, Virginia. She attended Spelman College in Atlanta, Georgia, before coming to Meharry. She was by far the most attractive and pleasant woman on campus. All of the guys liked Lei. I remember her for another reason: I sat next to her during the first exam we took in our freshman year. I kept staring at her huge, beautiful Afro hairstyle. Yeah, I flunked that exam. Later, in 1979, we also did our medical rotations together during internal medicine. Dr. Charlton now practices internal medicine in North Carolina.

At the end of our sophomore year of medical school, we took part in the National Medical Boards. The exam covered material learned in the first two years of school. We had about a month off to study. During this time, I formed a study group with my friends Norman Jones and Darrell Robinson. At the end of the morning sessions, we handed in the answer sheets and returned after lunch for the afternoon session. I handed my answer sheet to Dr. Burgess, who was about fifty-five years old and was much taller than I was. I gave him the papers and said, "This test is rough." He looked down at me and replied, "Life is tough." I thought to myself, *I'll get no sympathy from him.*

My surgery rotation in medical school was extremely challenging because to perform surgery, I needed steady hands. I studied with Gail Jones, who is also from New York. She attended the City University New York (CUNY), at Hunter College in Manhattan, and was sharp and very confident. After just one look, you could tell she was a New Yorker. Gail was a pleasure to work with, but she could be aggressive when she had to be.

When I scrubbed for the surgery, my spastic moves caused me to touch areas of my body that were not sterile, which in turn caused me to become contaminated. I had to resterilize myself, which entailed rewashing my forearms and hands and putting on a new surgical gown, gloves, slippers, and a mask.

During my rotation, I actually made it into the operating room only once. I assisted the surgeon as he operated on one of my patients. I hated being in the operating room. I would drool inside the surgical mask due to my poor gag reflex. Because my hands were spastic, I could never tie the mask, and we had to stand with our arms up and elbows bent as if we were in a praying position. I had to stand in place for approximately two hours, which caused fatigue in my legs. I could not put in sutures or close at the end of the operation.

I appreciate the talents and skills of surgeons and surgery, but for me, it was the most physically challenging rotation in medical school. I'm glad they did not waive that rotation for me. I went to the lectures and passed the midterm and final. I can always read a book and pass an exam or memorize lecture notes. If doing any technical procedure were a requirement for passing the surgery rotation, I would have never become a physician. The same can be said for other physicians who are disabled.

On the other hand, I loved obstetrics and gynecology (ob-gyn). I delivered a baby on my rotation. It was an exciting rotation for me. Because they needed the experience, the residents usually did the manual work themselves, but they taught me a lot while I watched, and I scored quite well on the exams. Meharry had a very strong ob-gyn department.

Dr. Henry Foster was the chairman of the ob-gyn department. He really took a liking to me. This was not because he had gone to school with my father at Meharry; he had not. In fact, he had studied medicine in Arkansas. He was delighted to see me make it to medical school. I may have been the first CP student he'd ever had, and he seemed especially proud of my accomplishments. This is just a guess, because we didn't talk about it, but I was a good student during that rotation. I took the obstetrics part of the rotation in a city hospital in Baltimore.

Rotation in Baltimore's city hospital was a tremendous learning experience. Cliff Becker, from Kansas City, was on the rotation with me. Cliff and I had a lot of fun on the rotation and learned a lot. Cliff was a Morehouse man. Morehouse College is geared to African American men. It rates in the top three of historically black colleges. Howard and Spelman make up the other two.

Many books have been written about prominent Morehouse men. Rev. Dr. Benjamin Mays, past president of the college; Rev. Dr. Martin Luther King Jr., civil rights leader; and Rev. Dr. Calvin Butts, president of State University of New York at Old Westbury, New York, and pastor of the Abyssinian Baptist Church in Harlem are three Morehouse men that come to mind. My nephews Jacques and Jelani graduated from Morehouse, and then Jacques graduated from Howard University School of Law. I have always looked up to guys who graduated from Morehouse, or "The House," as it is affectionately called.

My favorite Morehouse man is Dr. Audley Mackel, orthopedic surgeon. I met "Mack" on the football field in 1977, our freshman year of medical school. He was not just a classmate but also a role model of mine. Mack is from Chicago.

I took ten courses in chemistry, three courses in biology, and a year of physics. In the chemistry lab, I broke my share of beakers and flasks, but the professors never got upset. The Lord was really with me, because I never caused a fire or an explosion while working with the Bunsen burners. I could place a beaker of liquid on a mat on top of a flame. If any of the procedures were overly technical, I got assistance.

In quantitative analysis, we had to measure solid matter such as sodium chloride (table salt) to the third or fourth decimal point, and that required tremendous manual dexterity. Dr. Karp was my professor for this course. A chemist should have patience, and he was an extremely easygoing man.

My worst nightmare was writing term papers in the nonscience courses. To this day, the expression "term paper" gives me an uneasy feeling. I learned the importance of dealing with my fears and insecurities head-on. I knew these classes would pose a physical challenge to me. I did not master the skills required in these classes, but I took the courses and did not ask for pity. Thanks in part to these classes, I have learned not to back down from a challenge.

There is definite merit to learning your craft well. Beyond the immediate gratification of helping patients overcome challenges, I received long-term gratification when others recognized my efforts. When I left Elmhurst Hospital in 1997 as a staff physician, I received a plaque that read as follows:

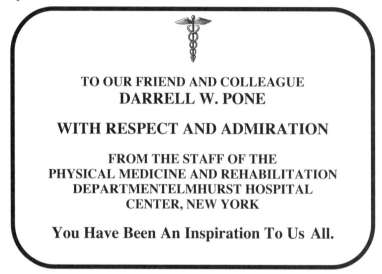

TO OUR FRIEND AND COLLEAGUE
DARRELL W. PONE

WITH RESPECT AND ADMIRATION

FROM THE STAFF OF THE
PHYSICAL MEDICINE AND REHABILITATION
DEPARTMENTELMHURST HOSPITAL
CENTER, NEW YORK

You Have Been An Inspiration To Us All.

KEY # 8: It is not enough just to be good. You must strive to be the best! It is important that you study hard and esteem yourself above the crowd. Les Brown, motivational speaker, always said, "Shoot for the moon, and you will land among the stars."

* Choose a learning institution that offers credentials in your chosen area of interest.
* Get a sound education, and take specialty classes as needed.
* Know your craft better than anyone. Do not focus on just one area.
* Learn all areas that are peripherally related to your work.
* Never be timid or avoid difficult challenges.
* To be successful, you must do the things that are hard. Anyone can do the things that are easy.
* The best way to learn your craft is to teach it to others. Tutor other students, or teach a class.
* Stretch yourself.

SUCCESS KEY #9
Pay Attention to Your Appearance. Many Major Decisions Are Based on Appearance.

Clothes and manners do not make the man; but when he is made, they greatly improve his appearance.
— Henry Ward Beecher (1813–87), American Politician

Image Is Everything

Image is everything—at least that's what people who are already established in their occupations tell me. One of my professors said this in medical school, as did the chairman of the department, Dr. Lawrence Freedman, while I was in residency.

Mom and Dad always told me that doctors are supposed to have a certain amount of etiquette, class, and style. During my life, Mom taught home economics in high school for about twenty years. At home, she taught us the proper way to sit at the table, hold a fork, and chew with our mouths closed. This was certainly a challenge for me. It was impossible for me to hold the fork and bring it to my mouth without dropping some of the food. My lips and tongue were spastic, and I drooled when I chewed. Even today, I smack my lips when I chew, and it is impossible for me to chew with my mouth closed.

I am invited to banquets, doctors' dances, and formal dinner dances. It is difficult for me because of my problems with spasticity. How I function is very important to me, so I have developed a system that works for me. I push my food onto my fork with my thumb instead of with a knife. I cannot cut chicken from the bone with a knife, so I use a combination of my fork and my hand.

Once, a woman who accompanied me to dinner complained that she didn't like my table manners. I explained both the neurology and the process by which I placed food into my mouth, as well as the chewing and swallowing. She insisted, "I do not care for your table etiquette, Dr. Pone." This happened that one time, and it has never happened to me again. Fortunately, most people around me understand and don't make an issue of my good manners.

I pride myself on certain points of etiquette. People say that I dress exceptionally well, and I do. I buy flowers for my wife. I tip at restaurants. No one can ever call me cheap. I keep my hair cut and my shoes shined, and I definitely keep my car washed. I strive to be a perfect gentleman in every area. I try to compensate for having CP.

However, I am not very good at accepting silly criticism from people who do not know the first thing about CP. People tell me I am a role model and then whine about my being slow. The reason I'm a role model is that I overcame CP to become a doctor. I am slow because I have CP.

In keeping with my career as a doctor, I make a real effort to follow the rules. I don't dress as quickly as some people, but I pay attention to all of the details. I love to wear cologne, and I make sure that I always have breath mints. My wife loves when I wear bow ties and suspenders. I try to dress to impress her. In keeping with the doctor's style, I do not wear jeans and sneakers to work. I am always dressed in a shirt, a tie, slacks, shoes, and a white lab coat. Wearing a shirt and tie, as I stated earlier, is a challenge, but I use a buttonhook.

I pride myself on the fact that I have, on many occasions, purchased clothes for Gloria. Having an eye for fashion definitely gives me an edge in life.

Even though my spasticity compromises my etiquette, I have developed strategies to compensate. In life, when one is weak in one area, it is important to compensate in another area.

KEY #9: You should always dress as if you have already attained your goal. Dress and act in a manner that complements whatever position you want. If you do, something divinely inspired will propel you into that position.

* Every situation in life has a dress code. Learn it and respect it.
* Table manners are important. You might have an interview over dinner!
* Find a hairstyle that fits your occupation, and discuss it with your stylist.

SUCCESS KEY # 10

Include Your Creator in All That You Do.

Trust in the Lord with all your heart; do not depend on your own understanding. Seek God's will in all you do, and God will direct your paths.
— *Proverbs 3:5–6*

My Church

The Congregational Church of South Hempstead is located in South Hempstead, New York. Our pastor, Rev. Patrick Duggan, is a graduate of Harvard University and New York Theological Seminary. My wife, Dr. Nixon-Pone, serves as the associate pastor. Gloria usually preaches once a month on the third Sunday, and Rev. Duggan and the other ministers serve the other Sundays.

Rev. Duggan is very tall with a great sense of humor. His sermons are timely, powerful, and very energetic. I am an usher in the church once a month. The congregation is the United Church of Christ denomination. Ours is a predominantly African American church in a European neighborhood, which is unusual. There are quite a few professionals in our church, including other medical doctors, college professors, and lawyers. We also have a judge (Brother Reggie Brantley), a doctor of social work (Alma Norment Martin), a doctor of education (Diatra Jones), and a number of college professors. I am also involved with the Men's Fellowship. We do the usual community work that most churches get involved in. I also give lectures on various topics in physical medicine and rehabilitation.

We have a dynamic youth fellowship, and some of the children are very interested in medicine. On the second Sunday the children's church department is responsible for leading worship service. One of the highlights of the service is when our organist, Mr. Nigel Gretton, plays a special version of my favorite hymn, the name of which is the title of this book. Mr. Gretton teaches music at St. John's University, in New York.

Deacon William Jefferson is one of my favorite people in the world. He is a retired high school teacher. He and I both love jazz. He loves Thelonious Monk, and he has given me the nickname "Straight No Chaser," which was one of Monk's favorite tunes. Every time I see Jefferson, he cries out my nickname.

Brother Calvin Powell, also known as the "Nut Man," sells nuts and gives all the proceeds to the church. Deacon Lipsey is a retired engineer, and Mrs. Lipsey is a great cook. I love her macaroni and cheese.

The other thing I like about the Congregational Church of South Hempstead is that the members take time out to socialize on Sundays immediately following the service. Leaving our straight-backed pews upstairs, we journey downstairs and sit at round tables and engage in friendly conversation. We talk about our work, our families, and current events. Sometimes we are served a full dinner with fried chicken, macaroni and cheese, salad, collard greens, and corn bread, as well as delicious cakes and pies and coffee. On Father's Day, the men of the church serve breakfast before the morning service. Usually the youth make one small group, the little children make another, and then the adults form various groups. This is a very special time of fun, relaxation, problem solving, and serious bonding. I love and hold in high esteem both my church family and my fraternity brothers.

Congregational Church of South Hempstead

Members with Pastor Patrick Duggan on the right

KEY # 10: It is important to believe in a higher power, something or someone much greater than yourself. If you do, your faith will guide you through difficult times. You should feed your faith and starve your fears.

* Develop a relationship with your Creator, and be consistent in your faith.
* Pray daily, because God answers prayers.
* Give praise for each level of accomplishment.

CLOSING THOUGHTS

In this book I have attempted to share how God has blessed me. I have outlined my successes, struggles, laughter, tears, and joy. My remarks were taken from key areas of my life.

I hope I have provided insight to the life of an African American born with cerebral palsy who became a board-certified medical doctor. If I am great or if I have accomplished some great things in my life, it has been because God placed great people in my path and I simply modeled what I was given.

I am very pleased that Nassau County Executive Tom R. Suozzi has appointed me to Nassau County's Office for the Physically Challenged Advisory Committee. In this capacity, I look forward to working toward developing important public policy in the areas of housing, health-care access, and employment opportunities for persons with disabilities. I will also continue to be supportive of the National Medical Association, United Cerebral Palsy of Nassau, the Congregational Church of South Hempstead, and the church as a whole.

This journey would have been impossible without my loving parents—my mother, Mrs. Annette Tulane Pone, and my father, the late Dr. Jesse J. Pone Jr.—my wife, Dr. Gloria Nixon-Pone, my mentors, my immediate and extended family, and my friends. I thank God for all of the people he placed in my path, whether they brought joy or pain. My life is an example of the African proverb "It takes a village." I understand that a lot of people will take exception to some of my words. But that is good.

I do not know what the future holds. God knows. I plan to keep on giving public testimony to my faith journey. I will continue to serve the wider community by speaking to inspire in the classrooms, churches, and professional and social organizations and to you in my book and by way of radio and television programming.

In the end, I am truly blessed. Only in America can an African American boy born with cerebral palsy grow up and become a physician and have the opportunity to practice medicine for more than twenty years.

As the psalmist wrote in chapter 116 and verse 3, "The cords of death entangled me, the anguish of the grave came upon me; I was overcome by trouble and sorrow." I truly believe that the Lord delivered me from death. I have lived a blessed life. With my spirit, mind, and body, I have attempted to walk before the Lord in peace and joy and love for all humanity. At this point in my life, I can truly say:

> [I've] come this far by faith,
> Leaning on the Lord.
> Trusting in His holy word,
> He's never failed me yet.
> Oh — can't turn around,
> [I've] come this far by faith.
>
> I pray that I won't be discouraged
> When trouble's in my life,
> He'll bear my burden and
> Move all misery and strife.
>
> I can truly say that God has made a way,
> And He's never failed me yet.

> — *African American Spiritual*

Our Deepest Fear Is Not...

"Our deepest fear is not that we are inadequate. Our deepest fear is that we are powerful beyond measure. It is our light, not our darkness, that most frightens us. We ask ourselves, who am I to be brilliant, gorgeous, talented, and fabulous? Actually, who are you not to be? You are a child of God. Your playing small doesn't serve the world. There is nothing enlightened about shrinking so that other people will not feel insecure around you. We were born to make manifest the glory of God that is within us. It is not in just some of us; it is in everyone. And as we let our own light shine, we unconsciously give people permission to do the same. As we are liberated from our own fear, our presence automatically liberates others."

—Marianne Williamson, in *A Return to Love*, 1992

Fifty Years and Counting

On May 12, 2005, I had a great day of celebrating my fiftieth birthday. I completely enjoyed myself. Of course all of the guys were there along with other friends dating back to kindergarten through medical school, and other practicing physicians showed up. My loving wife and mother, my sister, Cheryl, and my brother, Victor, participated in the celebration. Lar, Joseph, and my wife's family were in the house. My church family was there in great numbers with me also. The big fun in that is that now I make more time in my schedule to speak to children of all ages and encourage them to believe in themselves and to never, ever give up on their dreams and aspirations.

Walking has always been a challenge for me. Today my left hamstring is tight, and it is difficult for me to put my heel down on the ground. The heel on my left shoe is brand-new, because it never touches the ground when I walk. When the heel on my left shoe is compared to my right heel, the difference is telling. Additionally, the sole under my big toe on my left shoe wears out first. I have to be very careful in crowds, because one small shove will cause me to fall. As a child, I wore braces to give support for both feet and legs. I walked with a limp, and children would always stare at me. Some laughed. I felt very self-conscious. With many years of therapy, I am blessed to have learned the skill necessary to better manage drooling. Contrary to some opinions, I believe CP has been a great teacher. It has taken me on a learning expedition and has proven to be a tremendous blessing in disguise.

My fine motor coordination in both hands is, to some degree, still a challenge. With my hands being spastic, it is difficult for me to hold small objects such as a pen, toothbrush, fork, or knife. Also, I drool at times and have difficulty when chewing and swallowing. These difficulties may interfere with speaking, eating, and kissing.

Today, I still have some speaking challenges. Quite regularly I will speak too fast or too quietly, and my words are sometimes unclear because I have poor control of the muscle in my mouth. But I know I could have died at birth or been born mentally retarded or confined to a wheelchair. And I could have been totally dependent on another person for my daily care. So, it is definitely a blessing to be of a sound mind and be in possession of all of my mental faculties.

Now, the emotion I am working on is crying. To do this, I have learned to direct my thinking toward other topics—usually sports or music—whenever I have the urge to cry.

<u>Fiftieth Birthday Party</u>

Gloria & Darrell

Lauren, Gloria, Mom, Darrell, Cheryl, Victor
Lisa, Avery, Sara Grace

Fiftieth Birthday Party

Gloria, Mom, & Darrell

Bob Carter & Darrell

Dr. Alma Norment & Edward Martin

Daily Meditation

If you write your affirmation below, say it each day, and believe it, it will come to pass. Although you may stumble and may even fall, you will not stay down. You will have the strength to get up, dust yourself off, and overcome any obstacles you might face, and you will be stronger because of it. In the space provided, describe the innate desire of your heart. Make a copy, and place it where you will see it every day. Encourage friends to do the same daily meditation to get them on the road to accomplishing their dreams.

MEDITATION

MY MIND CONCEIVES AND

MY HEART BELIEVES THAT

I CAN BE A _____

THEREFORE, I, _____,

WILL ACHIEVE MY DREAM!

Note of Appreciation from Students

**Mrs. Miraglia Sill's First-Grade Class,
Park Avenue School, Westbury, New York**

The End

Endnotes

The Links Inc.

In November 1946 two black women, Margaret Hawkins and Sarah Scott, invited some seven friends over to form a new type of inner-city club. Mrs. Hawkins had actually conceived of this idea a year earlier in 1945 with friends along the eastern seaboard. They had envisioned an organization that met black women's needs and aspirations, namely civic, educational, and cultural. The club, the Links, would foster cultural appreciation through the arts, develop intergroup relations, and help women accept their civic and social responsibilities. The original Links also included Frances Atkinson, Katie Green, Marion Minton, Lillian Stanford, Myrtle Manigualt Stratton, Lillian Wall, and Dorothy Wright. They elected the following officers: president, vice president, recording secretary, corresponding secretary, and treasurer.

The Links are noted for their services to the black youth in America. At the Links Inc. Tenth National Assembly in 1958 under the Dwight Eisenhower administration, they pledged a "Talent Search" as a goal of a national program. "Educating for Democracy" was the theme. They were looking for academically talented youths. This was undertaken by all chapters. This program was to be pursued for four years. More than two thousand gifted youths were discovered between 1958 and 1962 under the "Education for Democracy" program.

The Links Inc. services to the youth focused on seven specific areas: teen pregnancy, juvenile crime and delinquency, alcohol and substance abuse, mental and emotional illnesses/disorders, breakdown of the family, unemployment, and education. Drug and alcohol abuse seemed to be an issue in all seven areas, so drug and alcohol abuse prevention was the primary focus between 1982 and 1984. Through "Youth Eighties Survival," they worked with black families to teach children how to discriminate against drugs and provide opportunities to develop positive self-esteem and a feeling of hope for the future. During 1988–99 the Executive Council of the Links approved a Self-Esteem Task Force. The purpose was to strengthen Project LEAD. Under this task force a partnership was formed with the Library of Congress in its national literacy campaign "1991 Year of the Lifetime Reader." Gladys Gary Vaughn, PhD, is the current president of the Links Inc. Under her guidance the Links responded to Hurricane Katrina in the following ways:

- All chapters were called upon to make financial contributions to the disaster relief fund.
- Disaster relief was coordinated by area directors.
- Hurricane relief coordinating chapters determined the kinds of supplies and services needed, and members in areas where the victims had been relocated to worked with area directors that supplied services.

United Cerebral Palsy of Nassau (UCPN)

The United Cerebral Palsy of Nassau Inc. (UCPN) association, founded in 1948, operates a comprehensive treatment and rehabilitation center in Roosevelt, New York, that has earned international recognition for innovative and high-quality programs. Many state-of-the-art services are provided in the Fortunoff Treatment and Rehabilitation Center and other areas of the facility. It was there that I received the first pair of braces for my legs and physical, occupational, and speech therapy. A partial list of the administration includes the following:

- Robert Masterson, President
- Robert McGuire, Executive Director
- Thomas Connolly, Executive Vice President
- Carmela Lage, President of the Council of Auxiliaries

Additionally, UCPN has numerous volunteers including computer technicians, electrical engineers, electronics technicians, and clerical assistants. Other volunteers help with reading, assist with meals, and walk clients to the center for various programs.

Alpha Phi Alpha Fraternity

Since its founding on December 4, 1906, Alpha Phi Alpha Fraternity Inc. has supplied voice and vision to the struggles of African Americans and people of color around the world. Alpha Phi Alpha, the first intercollegiate Greek-letter fraternity established for African Americans, was founded at Cornell University in Ithaca, New York, by seven college men who recognized the need for a strong bond of brotherhood among African descendants in this country.

The fraternity initially served as a study and support group for minority students who faced racial prejudice, both educationally and socially, at Cornell. The jewel founders and early leaders of the fraternity succeeded in laying a firm foundation for Alpha Phi Alpha's principles of scholarship, fellowship, good character, and the uplifting of humanity.

Alpha Phi Alpha chapters were developed at other colleges and universities, many of them historically black institutions, soon after the founding at Cornell. While continuing to stress academic excellence among its members, the fraternity also recognizes the need to help correct the educational, economic, political, and social injustices faced by African Americans.

For speaking engagements or book signing,
please contact:

Lar Watkins
Elegant Events by Lar & Associates
Post Office Box 110256
Cambria Heights, New York 11411
ElegantEventsByLar@Gmail.com
(718) 978-8005 (office)
(917) 880-7840 (mobile)

For upcoming events or to purchase additional
books, visit our website:
www.PoneInspirations.com